INTRODUCTION

Third grade is an important year in school; you will now be able to take standardized assessments. These assessments will help you and your Guide find out what you know and what you are ready to learn. You will learn more about the world around you by reading novels and learning challenging math problems such as multiplication and division. This year is also when you begin to become an independent student.

Ready, Set, Go! is a workbook that has been created to help you learn how to become an independent student. Since you are learning to become an independent student, you will master strategies to show you how to study, what to study, and how to take tests. This book will give you practical tips for time management, setting goals, studying, and taking tests to help you become the best student you can be. You will learn how to look at different types of test questions and organize them into tiny steps so that you will be better able to answer them when you encounter them on a test. Learning how to succeed as a student will help you in school now and in the future.

ARE YOU READY? GET SET! GO!

SECTION ONE

PREPARATION

WEEK 1

LESSON #1: Welcome to a New School Year!

Estimated Time: 10 minutes

Welcome to third grade! This school year is a very important one. In third grade, you will learn many important new skills that you will use throughout your life. You will learn how to become a better reader and writer, you will learn more about the world around you, and you will learn new math skills, like multiplication and division. You will also learn how to become more responsible for doing your own work, and you will take many important tests to show what you have learned. Every day, you will learn a new skill or sometimes a helpful tip that will help you to become a better student.

Write three new skills you hope you accomplish or learn about this school year.

1. _____
2. _____
3. _____

LESSON #2: The Importance of Homework

Estimated Time: 10 minutes

Each day, you and your Guide will explore new ideas in reading, math, science, and social studies. Sometimes, you will complete a lesson and activities with your Guide. Other times, you will need to complete work on your own to practice a new skill. This is usually called homework. Homework is extra practice for a skill you have just learned. It is important to always do your homework assignments so that you can master the skill you just learned. Completing an assignment on your own after learning the information helps your brain keep that new information in your head. When you do a homework assignment, you use parts of your brain that help you learn how to become an independent learner and thinker. Sometimes by doing homework, you will discover that something is difficult for you. Even though it may frustrate you, this is a good thing to know because you will then know what areas you need to practice more. One good skill to get in the habit of doing is to talk or write about what was hard about your homework assignment. If you thought that it was not hard, then you will want to write or talk about what was easy. Doing your homework will help you to become a better student!

Write a sentence to tell why it is important to do your homework assignments. Write a second sentence to explain why homework is sometimes frustrating.

_____
_____
_____

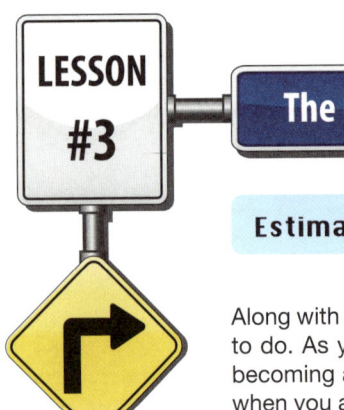

LESSON #3: The Importance of Tests and Studying

Estimated Time: 10 minutes

Along with completing homework assignments, learning how to study is very important to learn how to do. As you get older, studying is something you will always have to do. Studying is the key to becoming a successful student! Learning how to study now will help you become a better student when you are older. Throughout the year, you will learn many helpful tips to teach you how to study.

In every grade, there are tests you will have to take. Sometimes it will be something short, like a spelling test. Other times, it might be a longer test, like something called a standardized test. These tests usually cover more than one subject. You will learn more about different types of tests and how to take them throughout this school year. Studying and practicing new skills will help you become prepared to take all kinds of tests. The more you practice a skill, the easier it will become. This is exactly what studying does; it gives you the chance to practice skills over and over so that they become easy for you to do and to remember.

Does homework help you study? Why or why not?
_____
_____
_____
_____

LESSON #4: Finding a Place to Study

Estimated Time: 15 minutes

Where do you do your schoolwork every day? You might be sitting in a classroom at a desk with a teacher. Perhaps you are sitting at your kitchen table with a family member teaching you. Wherever you are learning, you will want to make sure it is in a quiet and well-lit area. It should also be free of distraction, or things that will keep you from paying attention to your work.

Trying to do schoolwork in a noisy room will make it very difficult for you to concentrate. For example, let's say you are trying to complete a page of math questions in your family room, but your little brother is watching his favorite television show about trains. He is probably jumping up and down, laughing, and having a good time. The TV is probably pretty loud, too. You are trying to solve the math questions on your paper, but you want to watch the trains on TV, and you are being entertained by your little brother. You aren't able to concentrate very well, and you start to make mistakes!

Now, let's say you are trying to complete that same page of math questions, but you are in your bedroom, sitting at a desk. There is a lamp on your desk, and the curtains are open, allowing bright sunlight to come through the window. No one else is around to make noise, and you are able focus and concentrate on the math questions on the page in front of you. You are able to complete the assignment quickly, and you get every single one correct!

DETOUR NEXT PAGE

END DETOUR ➤ The best place for you to do your schoolwork and study is a place that is fairly quiet, has good lighting, and is free of things to distract you, like a television. You will also need to make sure you have a desk or table to sit at and that you have a comfortable chair to sit in. Today, you will need to take the time to find a good place in your house to create a study area. Make sure that it is a place that follows these guidelines. Ask your family members to help you find a place to work. Make sure everyone knows this is your study area where you will be working. You may even want to make a sign to let everyone know this study area belongs to you! Once you find this place in your house, draw a picture of what it looks like below.

Briefly describe the space you chose as your study space. What rules did you set for the times when you will complete your homework?

_____
_____
_____
_____
_____
_____
_____

LESSON #5

Preparing Your Study Area

Estimated Time: 15 minutes

Yesterday, you found a place in your house that would be a good place for you to do homework and to study. Today, you will make this study area your own so you feel comfortable doing work there. If your area is a place that will be all your own, like a desk in your bedroom, you will be able to keep supplies right there on your desk. If your study area will be a place that other family members use, like in the kitchen, or if you are sharing a desk, you will want to have a box or container to store your supplies.

You will need to make sure you have the following school supplies in your study area so that you can find them as you need them:

- pencils
- erasers
- pencil sharpener
- highlighters
- crayons, markers, or colored pencils
- calculator
- scissors
- glue or glue stick
- notebook or scratch paper
- dictionary
- thesaurus
- calendar or school planner

Having these items at your fingertips will help you be able to complete your work quickly. If you did not have crayons at your work space, and need them for an activity, you would have to get up, search through the house for a box of crayons, and then try to refocus in order to complete your work. If the crayons are right there, you can reach for them and continue working without being distracted.

If you are working in your own space, you will want to organize your supplies in a way that makes sense to you. Maybe you have a special container for pencils and highlighters, a box to keep glue, scissors, and a calculator in, and a bookshelf to keep notebooks, a dictionary, and your school books stacked neatly.

If you are working in an area that you are sharing with other family members, you will want to use something to keep all of your school supplies together, like in a shoe box or other small container. This way, you can reach for your "school box" and have all of your supplies ready to go.

Collect all of these school supplies and organize them in a way that makes sense to you in your study area. Good organization is important in becoming a good student!

Check off what you have and make a list of what you still need. Be sure to let your family know when you will need to add supplies.

- ☐ pencils
- ☐ erasers
- ☐ pencil sharpener
- ☐ highlighters
- ☐ crayons, markers, or colored pencils
- ☐ calculator
- ☐ scissors
- ☐ glue or glue stick
- ☐ notebook or scratch paper
- ☐ dictionary
- ☐ thesaurus
- ☐ calendar or school planner

WEEK 2

LESSON #6: Making a To-Do List

Estimated Time: 10 minutes

This week you will learn some tips to help you stay organized and make time for schoolwork. This is often called time management. One more way that you can stay organized during the day is to make a to-do list. When you make a to-do list, you write down all of the things you must accomplish during the day. As you finish each task, you will cross it off your list. Then, you will be able to see what you still need to complete. There may be some things on the list that you want to accomplish today but you know you may not get to it. It's ok to put things on your list that may carry over to another day.

Here is an example of what a to-do list might look like.
Today, I need to:

- do language arts
- do math
- do science
- do social studies
- practice spelling words
- review math facts
- go to soccer practice
- rake the leaves

Make a to-do list for today. Each morning before you begin your lesson, make a to-do list to help you stay on track.

Today, I need to:

1. _____
2. _____
3. _____
4. _____
5. _____
6. _____
7. _____
8. _____
9. _____

Lesson #7: Set the Timer!

Estimated Time: 15 minutes

Sometimes when you are doing schoolwork, it may feel like the work will never end! You may think that it is better for you to work hard and not stop. But, it is actually very important for you to take a break every so often. Taking a break will allow your brain to make sense of the information you have just learned. It will also give you a chance to refresh yourself. Your brain is like a muscle that is exercising. Breaks help the muscle to get bigger and better!

A good rule of thumb is that for every thirty minutes you spend on schoolwork, you should take a five-minute break. This will allow you to get a snack, or a drink, and give your brain a rest. While taking your break, do not think about schoolwork.

To help you see when it is time to take a break, or tell when your break is over, you may find it useful to use a timer. You may use a timer on your watch, an egg timer, or a stopwatch. When you sit down to begin studying, set your timer for thirty minutes. When the timer goes off, it is time to relax! Set the timer again for five minutes and take a break. When the timer goes off again, it's time to get back to work.

Try this strategy today to see if it helps you to study better!

How would you know it is time to take a break? Write a sentence about some of the signs to look for when you are getting tired and need a quick break.

_____
_____
_____
_____

As you read, taking a break is important to allow your brain some time to rest after learning a lot of information. Some clues that you are ready for a break might include feeling tired, not being able to concentrate, needing to get a snack or a drink, or having to use the restroom.

LESSON #8

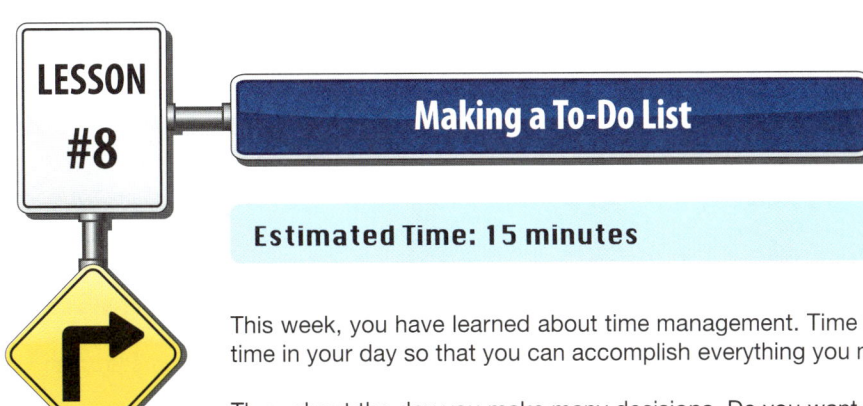

Making a To-Do List

Estimated Time: 15 minutes

This week, you have learned about time management. Time management is how you organize the time in your day so that you can accomplish everything you need to do.

Throughout the day you make many decisions. Do you want to wear a t-shirt or a sweater? Should you have apple juice or orange juice? Should you read a book or play a video game? Sometimes you make good decisions, and other times you might not make the best decision. Making the best decision when it comes to doing your schoolwork will help you have good time management.

During the day, you and your Guide set time aside to learn about math, science, social studies, and language arts. Are there things in your day that may affect when you can or cannot complete schoolwork? You will need to make sure to set time aside in your day to do the activities you have to do, like helping with chores around the house, or going to soccer practice. You will also need to set aside time to do homework or study. It is also good to have time in your day to do things you want to do, like watching TV or playing games.

By making a list of things that you must do during the day, like schoolwork, sports practice, or household chores, you will be able to see when you have time to do things you want to do, like spending time with friends, or playing video games.

Make a list of things that you have to do every day. Some examples might be school, homework, sports practice, club meetings, or chores. List the most important things first. Add more spaces if you need to.

1. _____
2. _____
3. _____
4. _____
5. _____
6. _____
7. _____
8. _____
9. _____
10. _____

Make a list of things you would like to do every day. Some example might be watching TV, going to a friend's house, or learning more about a hobby of yours.

1. _____
2. _____
3. _____
4. _____
5. _____

Tomorrow, you will use this information to help you make a daily schedule.

LESSON #9

Making a Weekly Schedule

Estimated Time: 15 minutes

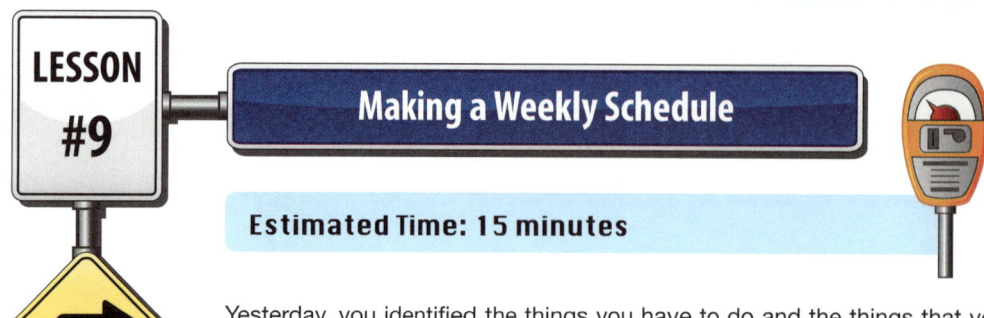

Yesterday, you identified the things you have to do and the things that you would like to do every day. Today, you will use that information to make yourself a weekly schedule. It is important to have a schedule. A schedule will help you make sure you do everything you are supposed to do and keep you from forgetting something important that must be done. It can also help you to see when you are busy and when you have free time.

Together, you and your Guide can make up your schedule. Use the weekly schedule workbook page on page 13. You will want to make sure all of the things you are responsible for, like chores and schoolwork, are on your schedule. You may also want to color code your schedule. Perhaps school is colored in blue, baseball practice is yellow, scout meetings are in green, and free time is in orange. When you are finished, hang your schedule in your study area so that you can refer to it when you need to.

An example is shown below.

Julianna's Weekly Schedule

	Monday	Tuesday	Wednesday	Thursday	Friday
8:00	Breakfast	Breakfast	Breakfast	Breakfast	Breakfast
9:00	Language arts	Language arts	Language arts	Language arts	Language arts
10:00	Language arts	Language arts	Language arts	Language arts	Language arts
11:00	Math	Math	Math	Math	Math
12:00	Lunch	Lunch	Lunch	Lunch	Lunch
1:00	Social studies	Social studies	Social studies	Social studies	Social studies
2:00	Science	Science	Science	Science	Science
3:00	Free time	Free time	Free time	Free time	Free time
4:00	Free time	Dance class	Free time	Dance class	Free time
5:00	Free time	Dance class	Free time	Dance class	Free time
6:00	Dinner	Dinner	Dinner	Dinner	Dinner
7:00	Free time	Free time	Girl scouts	Free time	Free time
8:00	Free time	Free time	Girl scouts	Free time	Free time
9:00	Bedtime	Bedtime	Bedtime	Bedtime	Bedtime

DETOUR NEXT PAGE

END DETOUR

_____'s *Weekly Schedule*

	Monday	Tuesday	Wednesday	Thursday	Friday

LESSON #10

How to Use a Calendar

Estimated Time: 10 minutes

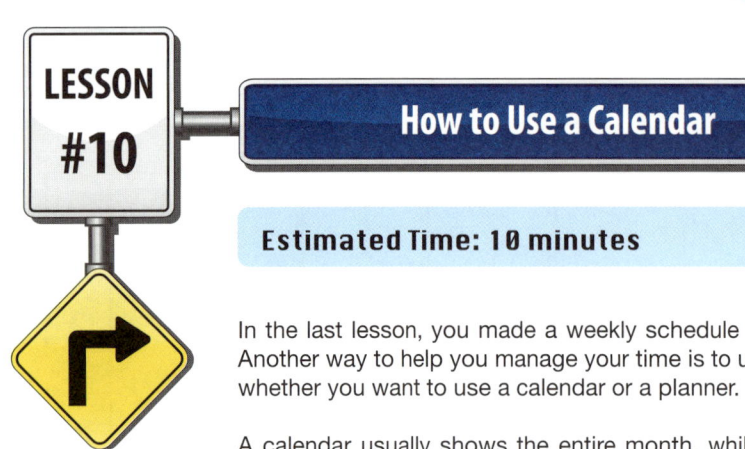

In the last lesson, you made a weekly schedule for yourself to help you keep track of your time. Another way to help you manage your time is to use a calendar or planner. It will be your choice on whether you want to use a calendar or a planner.

A calendar usually shows the entire month, while a planner may show just one week at a time. Choose the one that you like the best.

As your Guide gives you assignments or projects to work on, you will want to write these down on your calendar or planner. For example, if your Guide tells you that you will have a spelling test on Friday, you will want to write this down on the Friday block of your calendar or planner.

September

Sunday	Monday	Tuesday	Wednesday	Thursday	Friday	Saturday
1	2	3	4	5	6 Spelling Test!	7
8	9	10	11	12	13	14

Then, when you look at your calendar, you will be able to see when you have work that is due, or a test to study or prepare for. Occasionally, there will be time where activities or assignments may need to be rescheduled due to being sick or other things that may come up in the day. If you have to reschedule an event, make sure to erase the old calendar entry and write it in the correct place to help you from being confused. Review your calendar every couple of days to check for overlapping of times or days. Being able to see what schoolwork you have to do throughout the week will allow you to make time for other activities you want and need to do!

At the end of each school day, with your Guide, take a few minutes to go over any projects or upcoming tests you may have and write them in your planner. You will find that this helps to keep you organized.

LESSON #11: Why Should I Listen?

WEEK 3

Estimated Time: 15 minutes

Being able to actively listen and follow directions is one of the most important things you will learn in school. It is important to listen carefully and closely so that you are able to follow directions properly. When you are young, you listen to what your parents and teachers say, then follow the directions. When you are older you need to listen to what your boss says, then follow the directions. This is why listening and following directions are important! This week you will practice listening and following directions.

Good listening will help you to become a better student. When you listen carefully, it will be easier for you to remember the new information you are learning.

Here are three tips to help you become a better listener:

1. Look at the person who is speaking. Pay attention to the speaker, and make sure to make eye contact with that person. Making eye contact means to look that person in the eye.

2. Repeat what the speaker says. Repeating the important points will show the speaker you are paying attention and saying it out loud will help you to remember the new information easier. You may want to say it to yourself so you do not disrupt others around you.

3. Ask questions. If you do not understand what the speaker is saying, ask for more information. This will help you to better understand.

While listening to your Guide during today's lessons, make sure to use these tips. Try using these tips in other areas of your life, too!

List three additional qualities of a good listener:

1. *My eyes are looking at the person I am talking to.*
2. _____
3. _____
4. _____

LESSON #12

Using My Listening Skills

Estimated Time: 10 minutes

Today, you will practice listening skills. Your Guide will read you a series of directions. Use your listening skills to do exactly what your Guide tells you to do. For this activity, you will need crayons, markers, or colored pencils.

LESSON #13: Using Your Ears

Estimated Time: 15 minutes

In the last lesson, you practiced listening by drawing a picture. Today, you will practice listening again. You and your Guide will play "Simon Says." Your Guide will tell you something to do. You will do the activity only when your Guide says *Simon says.* If your Guide does not say *Simon says,* then do not do what your Guide says to do. When playing this game, you will have to listen very carefully, or you will be out! Try to use the listening skills of looking at your Guide and repeating the directions to yourself.

LESSON #14: Following Written Directions

Estimated Time: 15 minutes

Sometimes, you are given a direction verbally. This means someone tells it to you. Other times, you will have to read directions to yourself to figure out what you have to do. When reading a set of directions, whether it is on a test or while you are making cupcakes, you must follow them exactly. Imagine you are making cupcakes and the recipe calls for 1 cup of sugar. You think you don't need to do what the recipe says and you only put in ½ cup of sugar. After you bake the cupcakes, you decide to take a taste, yuck! The cupcakes are not very sweet, because you didn't add enough sugar. This happened because you did not carefully read and follow the directions! This is only one example of why it is important to carefully read and follow any directions that you are given.

When you read the directions to an assignment, or a recipe for a meal, or instructions for putting a model together, you may need to read the steps or directions more than one time. You may also find it helpful to underline the specific task you are asked to complete.

Use this strategy to complete the assignment below.

Every family is different. Some families only have one child, while others have many children. Some families live with aunts, uncles, or grandparents. Some families are only one parent and one child. Write three sentences about your family. Then, write one sentence about why your family is special.

Go back and reread the directions. Underline what you will do. Now, follow the directions that you just underlined and complete the activity below.

_____
_____
_____
_____
_____
_____

LESSON #15

Reading and Following Directions

Estimated Time: 10 minutes

You will be given directions in every area of your life. You read or hear directions when completing schoolwork. Your dad may tell you to clean your room. There are instructions to tell you how to play a game. Another place you will commonly find directions is in the kitchen. A recipe gives you the directions to make a delicious treat to eat! Today, you will follow written directions to make yourself a snack. Be sure to follow the directions in the recipe exactly so that you have a tasty treat to enjoy!

Trail Mix

Gather the following supplies:
1 cup measuring cup
½ cup measuring cup
Large bowl
Wooden spoon

Gather the following ingredients:
Cereal
Raisins
Chocolate chips
Peanuts
Small pretzels

Directions:
Step 1: Use the measuring cup to measure out 2 cups of cereal and pour it into the bowl.
Step 2: Measure 1 cup of raisins, 1 cup chocolate chips, and 1 cup of pretzels.
Step 3: Measure out ½ cup peanuts.
Step 4: Add the raisins, chocolate chips, pretzels, and peanuts to the bowl.
Step 5: Use the wooden spoon to stir the ingredients together.
Step 6: Measure out ½ cup of trail mix, and enjoy!

Makes ten ½-cup servings.

What other ingredient do you think would be tasty to add to your trail mix?

_____
_____

LESSON #16

Reading Written Directions

Estimated Time: 15 minutes

Before beginning an assignment, it is important for you to read the directions from beginning to end to make sure you understand what to do. If you don't read the directions fully before starting, you may miss something and do the assignment incorrectly.

Carefully read each direction below before starting this activity.

1. Write your full name in the top right hand corner of this page.
2. Write today's date under your name.
3. Draw a line through this sentence.
4. List each of your family members below:

   _____   _____
   _____   _____
   _____   _____

5. Draw a picture of your favorite animal.

6. Punch a hole through the lower right hand corner of this page.
7. Draw a big star in the middle of this paper.
8. Now that you have carefully read each of the directions, go back and complete only numbers 1 and 2.

What does your paper look like? Does it only have your name and date on it, or is there a hole in the paper and drawing all over it? If your paper only has your name and date on it, then congratulations, you know how to read and follow directions! If you have a hole in the corner and drawings everywhere, then you did not follow the directions. The very first direction said for you to read everything before beginning. The exercise was supposed to show you the importance of reading the directions before starting an assignment.

LESSON #17: Asking for Help

Estimated Time: 15 minutes

There are times that you will not understand what you are supposed to do or will need help with a certain topic. Maybe you find subtraction really hard, or maybe you read the directions on your reading assignment a couple times, and you still don't get it. What do you think you should do in these situations? Should you just ignore the work you are supposed to do? No. Should you just do it anyways and not care that it is wrong? Definitely not. Do you think you could ask your Guide or even a friend to help you? Absolutely! It is okay to ask for help! Asking your Guide to help you better understand a set of directions or show you how to subtract is the right thing to do. You could even ask a friend if he or she can help you. Many times two heads are better than one!

This week, if you come across something that you just can't figure out, make sure to ask for help.

LESSON #18: Where Do I Begin?

Estimated Time: 15 minutes

Imagine that you and your Guide have just finished your day's lessons. You have a spelling test in two days, some math problems to work on, and a story to reread. Which of these is your least favorite subject? Some students love math, but dislike reading. On the other hand, some students are really good at spelling, and like to read, but would prefer not to solve a page of math questions. You will probably want to do the subject you like the best first, but then what happens when you get to your least favorite assignment? Some students might grumble and groan, while others might make excuses for why they don't want to do that particular assignment. To help avoid this situation, you might want to complete the assignment you dislike first! By focusing on your least favorite first, you have the worst over with and you can focus your energy on it right away. Once you are finished with that dreaded assignment, it will be smooth sailing from there!

After today's lesson, decide the order in which you want to complete your assignments. Try to complete the one you like least first. Every day, this order might change, but you will find that you are more efficient when completing your work.

LESSON #19

What Should I Study?

Estimated Time: 15 minutes

You probably have a spelling test that you will need to take tomorrow, and you will need to review your spelling words at some point during today's school lessons. Which words should you study? The smart way to study is to briefly review your list of words and identify the ones that are difficult for you to spell. Then, focus your time and practice spelling the words that are hard for you to spell. By doing this, your brain will be able to focus just on these difficult words. Don't waste your time practicing what you already know.

This technique works well for all subjects, whether it is math facts, science concepts, or social studies information.

When practicing your spelling words for tomorrow's test, first identify the easy words and then the hard words. Then, spend your study time practicing the hard words. One additional way for you to practice hard to spell words is to write them each three times. Make it fun! Use different colored markers, type the words on the computer, or use your finger to write the words in a cookie tray filled with flour.

LESSON #20

Study Time

Estimated Time: 15 minutes

Setting time aside each day to study and review is very important so that you can learn the material in your lessons and do well on tests. Later in this book, you will learn many tips on how to study. Today, you will learn about the time you take to review and prepare for tests and quizzes. It is a good idea to break your study time into smaller portions. Studying for long periods of time without any breaks is not good for your brain. Your brain is able to handle small bits of information at a time. When you overflow your brain with a lot of information all at one time, not all of the information is retained, or kept.

Let's say you are preparing for a test in science. You think you will need about an hour to review the information and practice the material. Rather than stuffing your brain full for the entire hour, divide that hour up into four study sessions of only fifteen minutes. In fifteen minutes, you can reread information in the text. In another fifteen-minute study session, you can review the vocabulary terms. In the third fifteen-minute study session, you can review diagrams and charts. In the last fifteen-minute study session, review the last bits of information you may have missed. You could spread these review sessions over the course of a day, or over a few days. By breaking up your study and review sessions, your brain will be able to hold the information, and you will find that you do well on your test!

LESSON #21: Goal Setting

Estimated Time: 15 minutes

Setting goals is one way you can become a better student. A goal is something you work toward. You might use goal setting when you want to improve on something. For example, perhaps you have a hard time remembering certain addition facts. You might set a goal for yourself to be able to know the answer to each addition fact automatically. Then, you would take steps to make sure you attain, or get, to this goal, such as practicing facts every day, playing a computer game with math facts, and reviewing the facts that you struggle with the most. A goal can help you achieve something you once thought was difficult. Throughout this week, you will learn more about goal setting and begin to set some goals for yourself.

Can you think of any areas in your life, aside from school, where you might need to set goals?

_____
_____
_____

LESSON #22: The Importance of Setting Goals

Estimated Time: 10 minutes

In the last lesson, you leaned the definition of a goal. Today, you will learn why goals are important. People should continually set goals for themselves, whether they are related to school or another part of their lives. Goals help people to keep getting better in one area, and they can also help people to learn new things. For example, Leo might be a really good hockey player. Maybe he would like to learn a new sport. He decided to set a goal for himself to learn the rules of soccer and learn how to play the game. Once Leo meets his goal, he realizes he is an even better soccer player! Without setting this goal, Leo may never have realized that he is good at two different sports.

Why do you think setting goals is an important thing to do?

_____
_____
_____
_____

WEEK 5

LESSON #23: Steps to Set a Goal

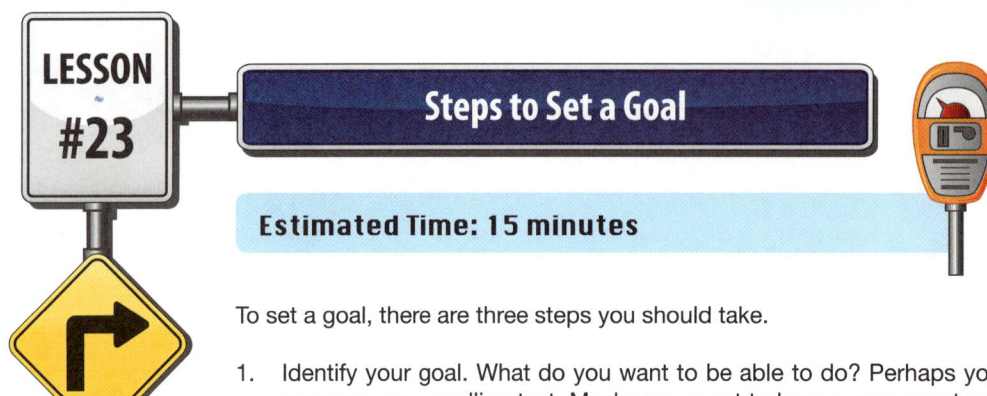

Estimated Time: 15 minutes

To set a goal, there are three steps you should take.

1. Identify your goal. What do you want to be able to do? Perhaps your goal is to get a perfect score on your spelling test. Maybe you want to learn a new sport or hobby, or you want to be able to keep your room clean all the time. Once you set your goal, write it down.

2. List the steps you need to follow in order to achieve your goal. If your goal is to get a perfect score on your spelling test, perhaps the steps you will take to that goal are setting aside ten minutes per day to just review spelling, playing different games to help remember the words, and taking extra time when spelling each word on the test. You should also write these steps down with your original goal.

3. Set a time frame. When do you want to accomplish your goal? Do you want to earn a perfect score on you next spelling test, or do you think that using the steps will help you to your goal in two or three weeks? Chose a time frame that is manageable. If you do not give yourself enough time to meet your goal, you may become frustrated with yourself and give up.

These three steps will help you to easily meet your goal. Tomorrow, you will begin to do some goal setting. Start thinking about what your goal could be.

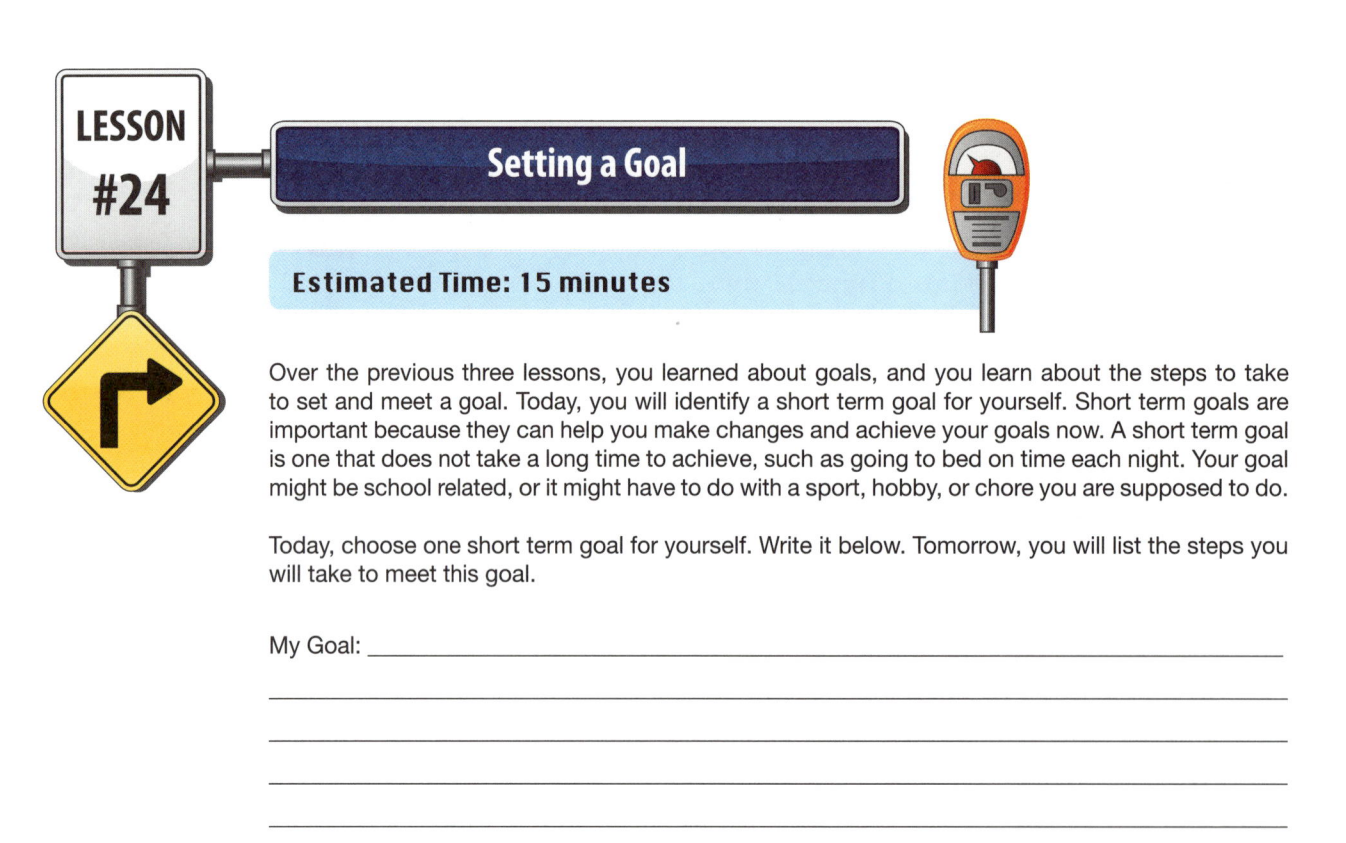

LESSON #24: Setting a Goal

Estimated Time: 15 minutes

Over the previous three lessons, you learned about goals, and you learn about the steps to take to set and meet a goal. Today, you will identify a short term goal for yourself. Short term goals are important because they can help you make changes and achieve your goals now. A short term goal is one that does not take a long time to achieve, such as going to bed on time each night. Your goal might be school related, or it might have to do with a sport, hobby, or chore you are supposed to do.

Today, choose one short term goal for yourself. Write it below. Tomorrow, you will list the steps you will take to meet this goal.

My Goal: _____
_____
_____
_____
_____

Lesson #25: Putting Your Goal into Action

Estimated Time: 15 minutes

In the previous lesson, you chose a short term goal to meet. Today, you will list the steps you will need to follow to meet your goal. For example, if you chose a short term goal of going to bed on time each night, the steps you might take to meet this goal are to finish your homework on time, turn the TV off at 8:00 p.m., and spend time reading in bed before turning the light out.

You will also want to set a time frame to meet this goal. Most goals will not be able to be met in just one day. Also, only meeting your goal one time does not mean your goal has been met. Goals can help you to make positive changes. If your goal is to go to bed on time each night, you would need to do this every night for at least a week to help form a new habit. Choose a time frame that you think is appropriate for you to meet your goal.

My Goal: _____

Steps to Achieve My Goal:

- _____
- _____
- _____
- _____

I want to accomplish this goal by: _____

WEEK 6

LESSON #26: Long Term Goals

Estimated Time: 15 minutes

Last week, you learned about goals. You even chose a short term goal and listed the steps you need to take to meet your goal. Have you started working on your goal? This week, you will learn about long term goals, and you will eventually set a long term goal for yourself.

As you remember from last week, a short term goal is something you would like to accomplish in a short amount of time. A long term goal is just the opposite. It is something that you would like to accomplish over a long stretch of time. It may take you a few months to a year or more to meet your long term goals. Some examples of long term goals might be scoring at least one goal by the end of the season, learning how to play a new instrument, or becoming a scientist. The last would be an extremely long term goal!

Long term goals are important because they help you to constantly make improvements in your life. A goal helps to keep you focused on what needs to be done.

Why are long term goals important for you to have?

_____
_____
_____

LESSON #27: How to Move Toward a Goal

Estimated Time: 10 minutes

Choosing a goal is personal. One person might want to focus on getting better in one particular subject, while another person might want to focus on getting better at a sport, or learning a new hobby. Once you settle on your goal, you will choose the steps needed to help get to that finish line. Perhaps one of your long term goals is to learn how to play the saxophone. There would be many steps to take to get to this end result. For example, you would have to:

- Learn how to read music notes.
- Find an instrument to rent or borrow.
- Learn how to blow into the mouthpiece.
- Learn the fingerings for each note.
- Practice every day to be able to play a song.

This is a long term goal because it is not something that could happen in a few days. It might seem overwhelming to keep track of each step. There are some things that you can do to help you make sure you keep working toward a goal. One way is to use a calendar. Once you choose your time frame, write that date on a calendar. Then, choose the dates you want to meet each of the steps on your way to the final goal. Write each of these on a calendar, and cross them off as you accomplish each step along the way. Using a calendar will help you to stay motivated to meet your goal!

LESSON #28

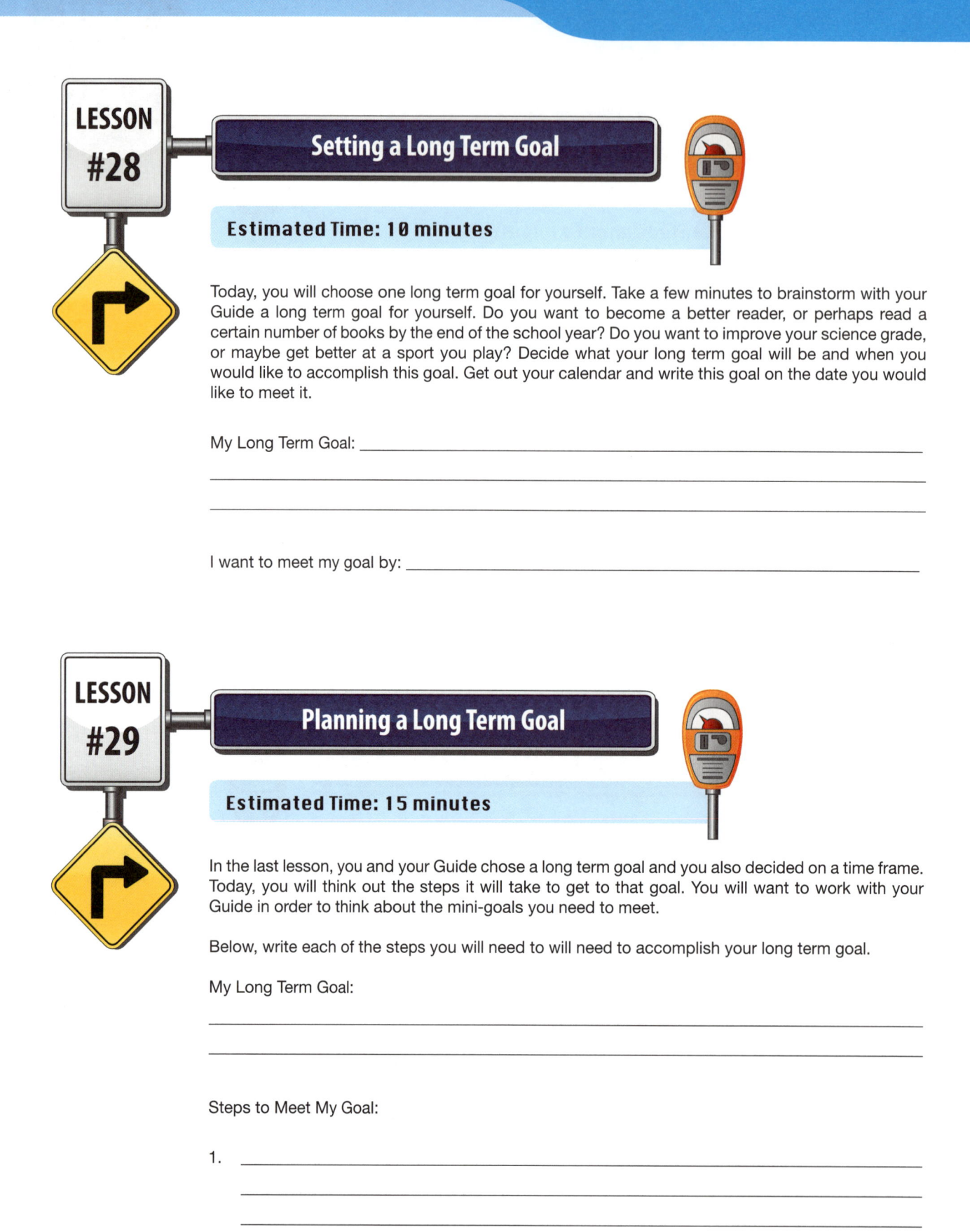

Setting a Long Term Goal

Estimated Time: 10 minutes

Today, you will choose one long term goal for yourself. Take a few minutes to brainstorm with your Guide a long term goal for yourself. Do you want to become a better reader, or perhaps read a certain number of books by the end of the school year? Do you want to improve your science grade, or maybe get better at a sport you play? Decide what your long term goal will be and when you would like to accomplish this goal. Get out your calendar and write this goal on the date you would like to meet it.

My Long Term Goal: _____
_____
_____

I want to meet my goal by: _____

LESSON #29

Planning a Long Term Goal

Estimated Time: 15 minutes

In the last lesson, you and your Guide chose a long term goal and you also decided on a time frame. Today, you will think out the steps it will take to get to that goal. You will want to work with your Guide in order to think about the mini-goals you need to meet.

Below, write each of the steps you will need to will need to accomplish your long term goal.

My Long Term Goal:
_____
_____

Steps to Meet My Goal:

1. _____
   _____
   _____

DETOUR NEXT PAGE

2. _____
   _____
   _____
   _____

3. _____
   _____
   _____
   _____

4. _____
   _____
   _____

5. _____
   _____
   _____

LESSON #30: Putting Your Plan into Action

Estimated Time: 15 minutes

Over the past two days, you have chosen your long term goal and the steps you will need to follow to accomplish your goal. Today, you will need a calendar to plan out your mini-goals to get you to your big goal.

You will start with the main goal on your calendar. Two lessons ago, you should have decided the time frame it will take you to accomplish your goal. Write your goal on this date on the calendar.

Next, look at each of the mini-goals you will need to accomplish on your way to your main goal. With your Guide, decide how long it will take to meet each mini-goal. Write each of these on the calendar. For example, if your goal is to read twenty-five books by the end of this school year, on your calendar, write this on each day you plan to read. You may also want to add how long you would like to read, in hours or minutes.

As you begin to work toward your goal, use this calendar to help keep you on track. When you meet one of the mini-goals, cross it off, and keep working toward the next goal. This will help to make sure you meet your goal on time!

WEEK 7

LESSON #31 — Prereading Skills: Skimming

Estimated Time: 15 minutes

This week, you will learn about some different techniques you can use to become a better student. Many of these techniques can be used while you read or study. There will be many times where you will need to read a textbook to learn about a certain topic. Some books may be online, while others may be a real book. For example, in social studies you might learn about the American Revolution. One way you can learn about this time in history is to read in your social studies textbook.

Instead of jumping right into your textbook, before you read you will want to use a technique called skimming. Skimming the pages you are supposed to read before actually reading them will give you an idea of what you will read and learn about. This helps your brain to think about this subject. If you will read about the American Revolution, and you have skimmed the pages in your textbook on this topic, you may start to think about everything you already know about this subject.

To skim material, you will look over the pages you are supposed to read, whether the book is online or offline. Look at the pictures, charts, graphs (if there are any), and any words that might be highlighted or bolded. Ask yourself if you know anything about this topic. If you do, start to think about what you already know. If you do not know anything about the topic, skimming the material before reading will give you the opportunity to start thinking about the new topic!

Today, before you read any new material in your textbooks, make sure to skim and quickly look over the information first. Skimming information before reading it in detail gets your brain ready to learn.

LESSON #32 — Using the Textbook To...

Estimated Time: 10 minutes

Yesterday, you learned how to skim your textbook to get ready to read. Another way to get ready to read is to look at the headings and images in the book. As an example, you may have been assigned to read four pages in your social studies textbook. Before jumping in to read, skim the material first to see what you will read about. Look at the pictures. Many times the pictures will give you a clue as to what you will read. If there are charts, graphs, or diagrams, look at these as well. These will also give you a really good idea of what that section will be about. Most textbooks will have a heading for each new section. The heading is a title that tells you what the next couple paragraphs are about. In a chapter on plants, there may be headings on life cycle, basic needs, and adaptations. By looking at these headings, you know that you will learn about how plants grow, what they need to live, and how they might change. This might get your mind thinking about one time when you planted flower seeds, watered them every day, gave them sunlight, and watched them grow. You can use what you already know to help you better understand what you are reading. The next time you are getting ready to read in a textbook, make sure to look at the headings. You will be surprised at how much more you understand!

LESSON #33: Prereading Skills

Estimated Time: 15 minutes

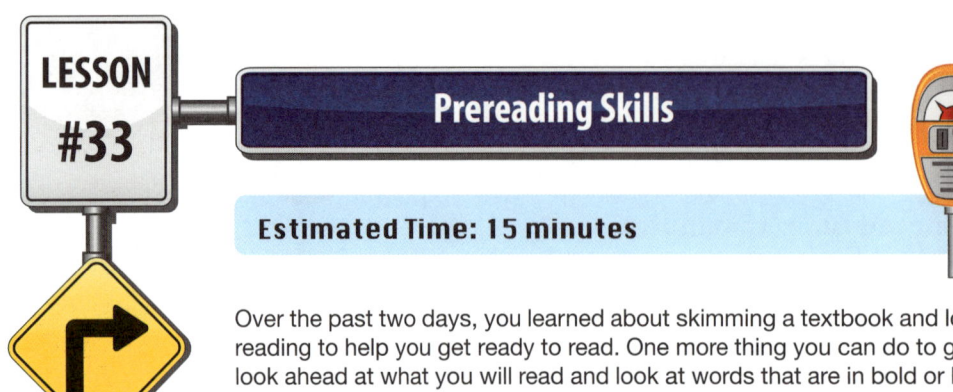

Over the past two days, you learned about skimming a textbook and looking at the headings before reading to help you get ready to read. One more thing you can do to get yourself ready to read is to look ahead at what you will read and look at words that are in bold or highlighted. These are usually the new vocabulary words that you will learn. Do you know what these words mean or how to say them? Look at the illustrations. Think about what is in those pictures. Do you know what the pictures are? If you know about the words or pictures, you can make connections in your head about what you already know about a topic and what you will learn. Looking ahead at the information in a textbook before reading is one more way to help you better understand new material.

Name three things you should do before reading a textbook.

1. _____
2. _____
3. _____

LESSON #34: Summarizing What You Have Read

Estimated Time: 15 minutes

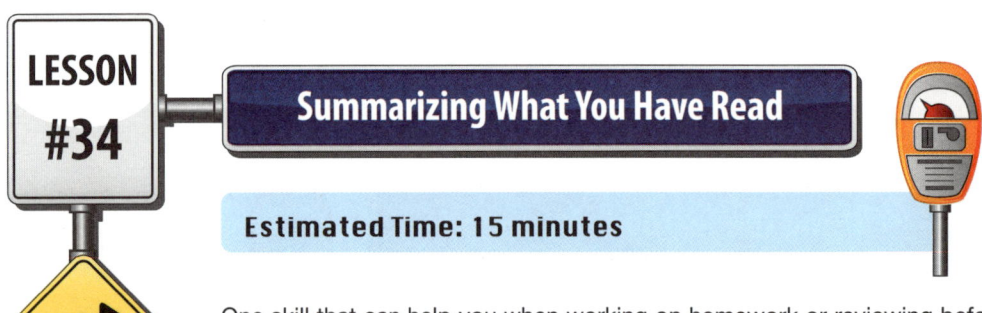

One skill that can help you when working on homework or reviewing before a test is summarizing. Summarizing is retelling what you have learned in just a sentence or two. A summary gives the main idea. You can use summarizing to help you remember the main ideas of what you have read. To do this, you will read the whole paragraph. After you have read the whole thing, ask yourself: *What was this paragraph about?* You may need to go back and reread what you have already read. Your answer to this question is your main idea. Adding a few of the main details to the main idea will give you a summary.

Read the following paragraph:

> This summer, Momma took a class to be a nursing aide. A nursing aide is sort of like a special helper for nurses. Most people call it a CNA, which is good because that fits much better on a nametag. Momma thought it would be easy to get a job as a CNA. Pittsburgh, the city where we live, is jam-packed with hospitals. But it's been over a month now, and Momma is still stuck at her old job as a hotel cleaning lady. It has made her a bit of a grouch lately.

What was this paragraph about? It was about Momma and how she is still looking for a job in a hospital as a nursing aide. This is a short summary of the paragraph. It was just one sentence to give the main idea of the paragraph. When reading in your books or textbooks, you can give a short summary at the end of every couple of paragraphs to help you remember what you just read. This will also help you remember the information for any tests you might have.

DETOUR NEXT PAGE

END DETOUR

Read the following paragraphs and give a brief summary.

> About twice a day, Ella goes absolutely bonkers and sprints around the whole apartment. I mean rocket ship fast, like a blur of growling fur. She lowers her body close to the ground and dashes in and out of every room, over and over. After a few minutes of total madness, Ella stops in the living room and basically falls over with a thud, totally wiped out.
>
> She started it this past winter. The first time I saw it, I thought my puppy had lost her mind. I thought she'd gone crazy and we would have to give her away, or at least buy her special medicine for her brain or something. I was so worried that I called Dr. Vanderstam myself. The address and phone number for his clinic is printed on the back of Ella's dog tags.
>
> He told me that Ella's weird habit was not actually that weird. Most dogs do it. It's a way they like to burn off their extra energy. It even has a name. It's called *the zoomies.*

Write a two sentence summary of what you just read.

_____
_____
_____
_____
_____

Your summary should have included the main ideas—the most important events or ideas in the passage. If you had trouble coming up with the main ideas, you can ask yourself who the main characters are, what are the big things he did, said, or thought.

LESSON #35: Rereading for Understanding

Estimated Time: 15 minutes

One way to help you understand the information you read in books or textbooks is rereading. Reading information just once is not always enough for your brain to remember the important parts. After you have read a few paragraphs, you should stop and summarize what you have just read. If you cannot retell what you have just read, you should go back and reread those last paragraphs. Reading the material again should help you to understand what you have just read.

Read the following paragraph:

> Temperature can affect air pressure. Cold air is heavier than warm air and presses against you more than warm air does. Heavy, cold air forms places of high pressure called highs. High pressure areas have clear skies. Warm air forms pressure areas called lows. Low pressure areas usually have cloudy skies. Wind travels from high pressure areas to low pressure areas. The bigger the difference in pressure between the two fronts the more wind that is produced at a greater speed. A sudden change in air pressure usually means that the weather is going to change. If the pressure drops it usually means that warm, moist high pressure air is moving in.

DETOUR NEXT PAGE

END DETOUR What is this paragraph about? Did you understand what the author was saying? If you did not, then go back and read it again.

Now that you have read this paragraph twice, are you able to give a summary of what it was about? Tell your Guide a brief summary of this paragraph.

Rereading is another skill that can help you to become a better student. The next time you aren't sure what you just read, take a moment to go back and reread the information. This will help you to better understand what you are learning about.

LESSON #36: Using a Highlighter

Estimated Time: 15 minutes

Last week, you learned many things you can do before reading to help you better understand what you will read. This week, you will learn about things you can do during and after reading to make sure you understood what you read. One thing you can do during reading is highlight information you find important. It is very easy to think that everything in a paragraph is important and highlight everything! Highlighting everything wouldn't help at all. When you highlight the most important sentence in a paragraph, you are making that idea stand out, making it easy for you to go back and review the main concepts.

After you read a few paragraphs, stop and ask yourself: *What was that about?* If you can give an answer, go find those few sentences in the paragraphs you just read and highlight them with a highlighter. If you cannot tell what those paragraphs were about, go back, reread, and then find the main idea.

Let's look at an example of how to do this.

> *Weather* is the condition of the air at a certain time and place. The weather can change from day to day. One day the weather may be windy and rainy. The next day the weather could be sunny and warm. People check the weather to know what it will be like outside so that they can choose their clothes and activities accordingly. For example, it's probably not a good idea to go to the park on a rainy day.

What is this paragraph about? It is about what weather is and different types of weather. The main idea of this paragraph is the following sentence: *Weather is the condition of the air at a certain time and place.* This is the sentence you should highlight.

> ==*Weather* is the condition of the air at a certain time and place.== The weather can change from day to day. One day the weather may be windy and rainy. The next day the weather could be sunny and warm. People check the weather to know what it will be like outside so that they can choose their clothes and activities accordingly. For example, it's probably not a good idea to go to the park on a rainy day.

When you go back to review before a test, you can look at the highlighted information to get the main ideas that will most likely be covered on a test.

Read the paragraphs below. Highlight the main idea in each of these paragraphs using a highlighter. You should highlight only three or four sentences. Remember, these should be the most important sentences that you have read.

> *Climate* is the weather of a place over a long period of time. The climate of a place is based on averages taken over a wide range of time, so it does not change often. The climate of a place includes the changes that happen as the seasons turn. It is important for people to know the climate where they live so that they can prepare for the weather. Farmers learn about the climate of a place so they know which crops to plant and when to plant them.

DETOUR NEXT PAGE

END DETOUR

Both the temperature and the precipitation of a place affect the climate. *Temperature* is how warm or cold a place is. The temperature can vary in different places. For instance, the temperature in Florida is mostly warm all year, while in Alaska it is mostly cool all year. *Precipitation* is the amount of rain or snow that falls in a place. In Texas it rarely ever snows, yet in New York it usually snows every winter. It is important for people to know these characteristics about where they live so that they can be prepared for any type of weather that may come.

Go back and review only the sentences you highlighted. The sentences you highlighted should be the most important ideas in the two paragraphs. Reading just those highlighted sentences should give you the main idea of the passage.

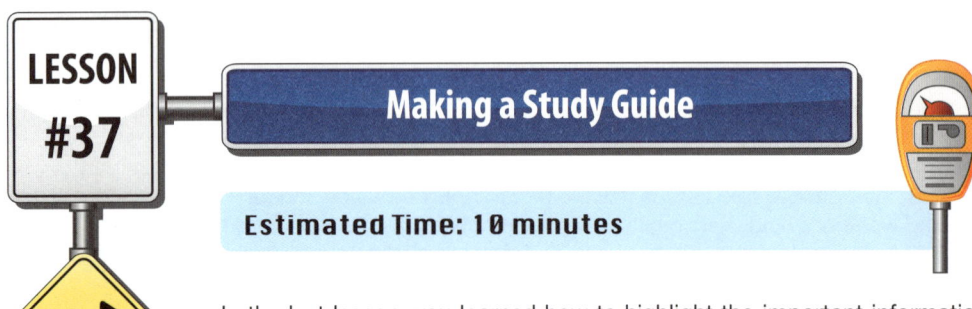

LESSON #37

Making a Study Guide

Estimated Time: 10 minutes

In the last lesson, you learned how to highlight the important information in a paragraph. Finding and highlighting the most important information in a textbook will allow you to go back and review the main ideas before a test.

Some of your books may be regular textbooks and you can use a regular highlighter pen to highlight the correct information. Some of your textbooks may be online. If this is the case, you can print out your book and then highlight it. You may also be able to use the highlighter function in your word processing program to highlight an online text. Whichever way you are highlighting, remember not to pick up or touch the highlighter until you have read a few paragraphs and decided what you need to highlight.

Read the paragraphs below and highlight the most important information. You should only highlight three to four sentences at the most.

When winds move fast enough, a hole develops in the center and a hurricane is formed. The word *hurricane* comes from Hurakan, the name for the Mayan god of the big winds. A *hurricane* is a dangerous spinning storm where winds howl and rain pours. The eye, or the center, of a hurricane is about ten miles wide and the storm surrounding the eye can cover up to sixty miles wide. The eye of the hurricane is calm, but the surrounding area is dangerous with winds around 150 miles per hour. Hurricanes can sometimes stick around for over a week and travel tens of thousands of miles over land and water. Hurricanes begin when warm air rises over 6,000 feet. The water vapor condenses and turns into rain drops, this releases heat energy. This movement of air forces air to rise up to about 50,000 feet and form cumulus clouds. The air from outside the hurricane tries to replace the rising air and causes the winds to begin to swirl. The updraft brings huge amounts of air and water vapor from outside the eye.

Hurricanes move in a counterclockwise motion in the Northern hemisphere and clockwise in the southern hemisphere. They are called cyclones in the Indian Ocean, typhoons in the Pacific Ocean, and willy-willies in Australia.

LESSON #38: Using Sticky Notes to Take Notes

Estimated Time: 15 minutes

Some students don't like to use highlighters to take notes. An alternative to highlighting is to use sticky notes. The point to using sticky notes is the same as highlighting; you want to make sure to write down only the most important ideas. You can then put the sticky notes in your textbook on that page. Or, if your textbook is online, you can then put these notes either in a notebook, or another place to help you remember the main points of what you just read.

After you read a few paragraphs, stop yourself and ask: *What were those paragraphs about?* Your answer to this question is what you will write on your sticky note. You can write either the actual sentences from the text, or you can write your summary on the sticky note. Then, you can refer back to your sticky notes to help you review the main ideas before a test.

Let's look at an example of how to do this.

> No two word problems are exactly the same. Because of this, your explanations will always vary depending on the problem. Some problems have several steps while some have only one. Some problems have more than one answer. Some problems require a lot of work, while others are mostly logical. There may be more than one way to solve a problem, so you need to include both. The sky is the limit!

What is the main idea of this paragraph? The main idea is that there are many ways to solve a word problem, and your explanation to how you solved the problem will be different every time you answer. On a post it, you might write:

> My explanation to a word problem may be different each time I solve a problem because there are many different way to solve a problem.

The sticky note can then mark your textbook page, or you could put it in a notebook.

Get a few sticky notes. Read the paragraphs below. Write a few main ideas on each note. You should only write three to four sticky notes.

> When you find a book or other resource that you would like to look at, you can either read it there or borrow it to take home. Most libraries have tables, chairs, and sometimes even couches for people to sit and read or study. If you would rather take the book home to read, then you have to check it out. First, you would need a library card. These cards are usually free and just give you an account at the library. This way the librarians can keep track of the people who have borrowed their books. You can borrow them for a short period of time, and then you have to return them back to the library.

> Public libraries will often have a separate section or room just for children! All of the children's books and resources will be located in that area. They also sometimes provide a storytime. This is when a librarian or other volunteer will sit and read books to the children who come to listen. Any child in the community is invited to join in storytime!

LESSON #39

Using Pictures to Understand

Estimated Time: 10 minutes

In any kind of book, you will often find illustrations. An illustration may be a picture, drawing, or diagram. All of these can help you to better understand what you are reading. For example, in a chapter on plants, there may be pictures of specific plants, diagrams of a plant's life cycle, and drawings of the inside of a seed. All of these can help you to see what the author is trying to tell you. It helps you to get a better picture in your mind. When you see an illustration, don't just skip over it. Look at the picture and read the caption below it. If you need to, go back and read the paragraph next to the picture to help you make a connection between the text and the picture. The pictures are in the book to help you!

Look at this example:

> The new moon is when we don't see anything, then it goes to a crescent moon, to a first quarter moon, full moon, last quarter moon, and back to a new moon. Look at this diagram for a better understanding of the moon phases.

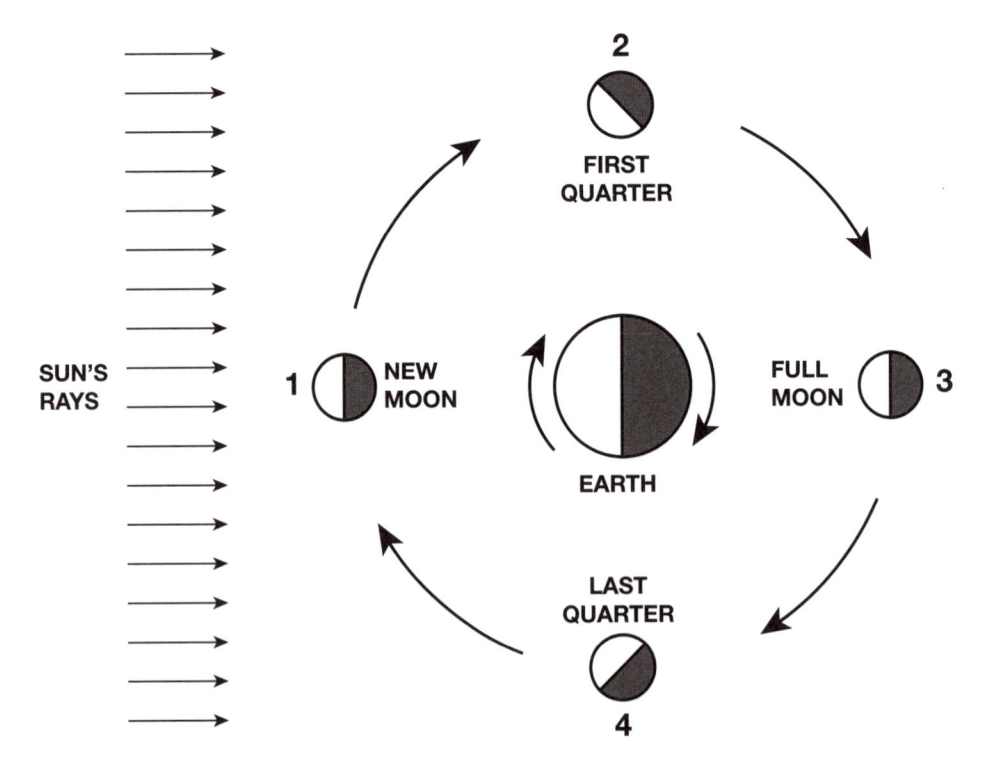

The illustration of the different phases of the moon helps you to get a picture in your head. If you just read that paragraph and there weren't any pictures, you might have a hard time trying to understand what the author meant. But, when you see the images of the different moon phases and read the information you should better understand each of the phases.

When reading in your textbooks, make sure to carefully look at the pictures that go along with each section. These pictures are there to help you understand.

LESSON #40

Using Graphs and Diagrams

Estimated Time: 15 minutes

Just like pictures, graphs and diagrams are put into textbooks to help you better understand what you are reading. Reading information and seeing it in a visual, like a graph, helps your brain to remember what you have just read.

When you come to a graph or a diagram, take a few minutes to read the information in the image. Do not skip over it.

In a lesson on the layers of the earth's crust, you may see a diagram like this:

Earth's Interior

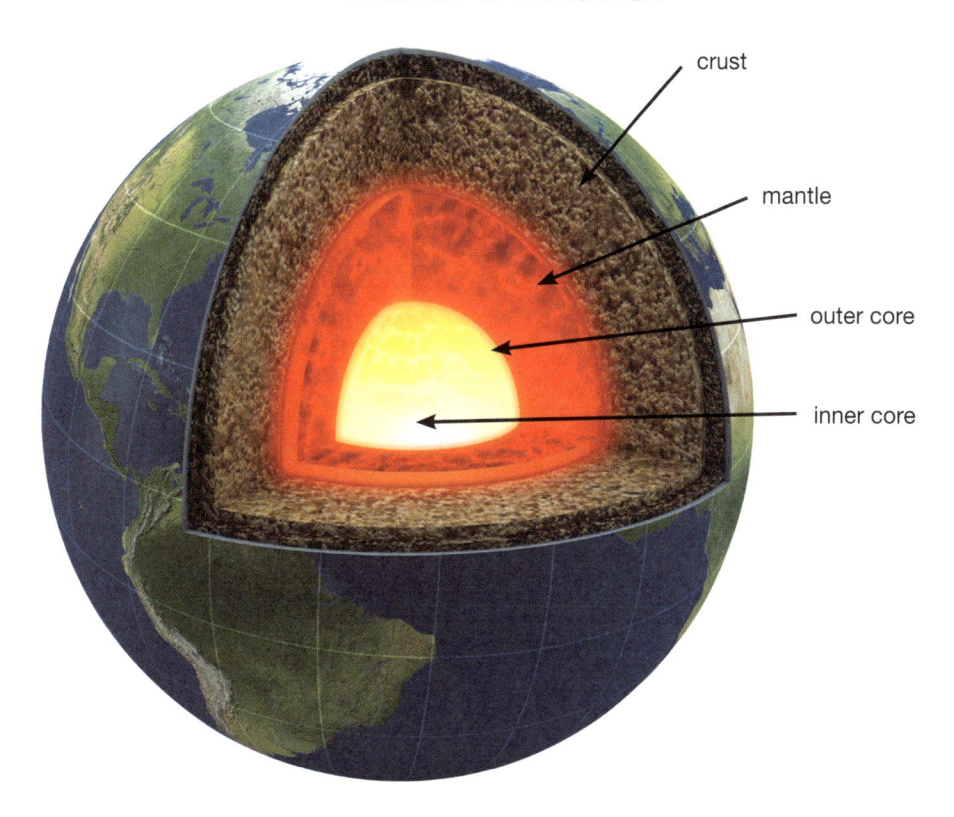

- crust
- mantle
- outer core
- inner core

This diagram shows each of the layers of the earth. Just reading the information is not enough to help you understand what the author is saying. A diagram showing each layer helps you to make the connection between the words on the page and the ideas in your head.

The next time you come to a picture, diagram, chart, or graph, make sure to take a few moments to look and read the information shown in it.

Why should you look at the pictures, diagrams, charts, or graphs in a textbook?

___
___
___

WEEK 9

LESSON #41: Post-Reading Strategies

Estimated Time: 10 minutes

You have learned some strategies to use before and during reading that can help you understand and better remember the information you read. After you read, there are some activities you can do to help you to remember what you have just learned.

- In a notebook, jot down any questions the information has made you think of. Then, look up your answers in another book or use a reliable source on the Internet.

- Have a discussion with your Guide about what you just learned. Talk about things you found interesting, need more help with, or want to learn more about.

- Briefly review the information you highlighted or wrote down on sticky notes. Immediately reviewing the main ideas of what you just read helps you to remember it better.

These three strategies can help you better understand and remember the information you learn as you read in your books and textbooks. Use these strategies time you finish reading.

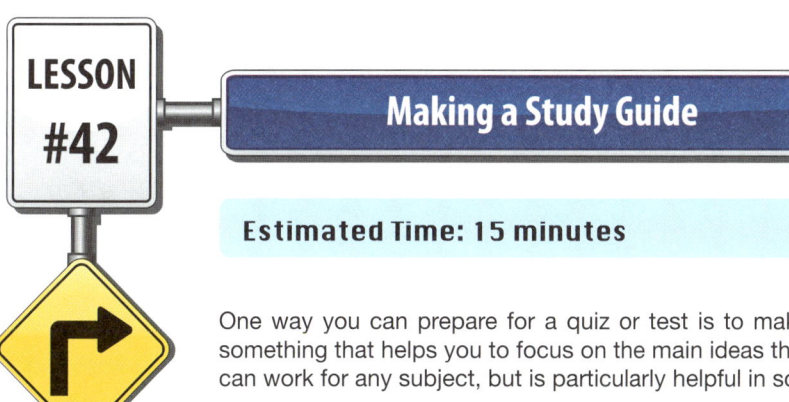

LESSON #42: Making a Study Guide

Estimated Time: 15 minutes

One way you can prepare for a quiz or test is to make your own study guide. A study guide is something that helps you to focus on the main ideas that might be covered on a test. This strategy can work for any subject, but is particularly helpful in science and social studies.

When you create your own study guide, you will look over the material you have just learned. You can use the material you are reviewing to make your own test questions or even a review game. All of these things help you to review, remember, and prepare.

To make your own study guide, look over the material that will be covered on your next test. For example, perhaps you have a science test coming up on rocks and minerals. Look at the information in the textbook with your Guide. Look at the information you may have highlighted as important. Can you make a test question out of that highlighted information? For each paragraph, you should try to make two questions. Once you have written the questions for that section, try to answer them without using your text. After you have answered the questions, you can check yourself by using your textbook.

Let's look at how to make a study guide from a few science paragraphs.

DETOUR NEXT PAGE

END DETOUR

Igneous comes from a Latin word, *ignis,* which means fire. *Igneous rock* is rock that forms when melted, or molten, rock from the earth's mantle cools and hardens. Remember, deep inside the earth it is extremely hot. Such temperatures can cause some rock to melt. This melted rock is called magma. When this melted rock cools, it forms igneous rock. Sometimes the melted rock flows from an opening in the crust to the surface of the earth. These openings are called volcanoes. Molten rock that reaches the surface of the earth is called lava. This molten rock, or lava, that comes to the surface contains different minerals and cools quickly, forming crystals. Formed crystals are very small. One type of igneous rock is a diamond.

1. This type of rock is made from molten rock that is cooled and hardened.

2. What is another name for melted rock?

3. How does molten lava escape from the earth?

4. Name one type of igneous rock.

From this one paragraph on igneous rocks, four potential test questions were made. Choose the most important details and make a question out of it. Once you have written the questions for that section, try to answer them without using your text. After you have answered the questions, you can check yourself by using your textbook.

Read the two paragraphs below. Make a mini study guide. Make at least two questions from each paragraph.

Another type of rock is sedimentary rock. *Sedimentary rock* is rock that forms when sand, particles of rock, soil, and other pieces of sediment harden. Wind, moving water, and moving ice can cause erosion or break large rocks into smaller pieces. The smaller pieces of rock are carried away by water or wind and then dropped in layers. As time passes, these layers become very deep. These layers stack on top of each other and become sedimentary rock. The type of sedimentary rock that forms depends on what materials the rock is made up of. For example, sandstone contains sand particles.

The last type of rock is metamorphic rock. *Metamorphic rock* forms when existing rock is changed by heat, pressure, or chemicals. These changes happen under the earth's surface. Igneous and sedimentary rock can change into metamorphic rock, and metamorphic rock can also change into a different type of metamorphic rock. An example of metamorphic rock is marble.

1. _____

2. _____

3. _____

4. _____

LESSON #43

Studying Vocabulary Words

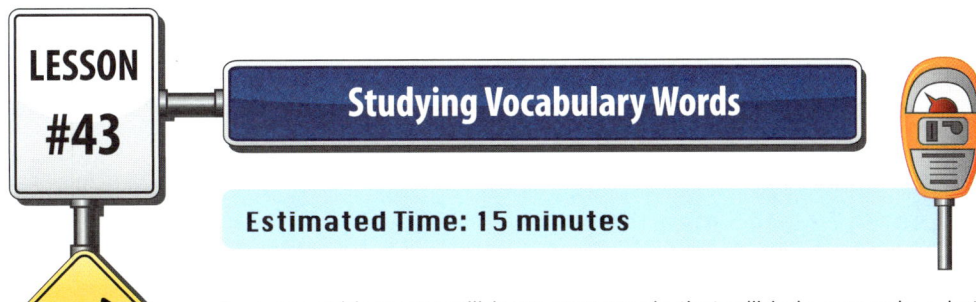

Estimated Time: 15 minutes

In every subject you will learn new words that will help you gain a better understanding of that subject. These new words are often called vocabulary words. In reading, they may be new words in a story. In math, you have vocabulary words that tell you about the parts of a problem. In science and social studies, the new words you learn teach you about the world all around us.

There are many ways you can learn the words and their definitions, or meanings. One way to do that is by making flashcards. On the front of the card, you will write a vocabulary word. On the back of the card, you will write the definition. For example, if a vocabulary word in science is *precipitation*, you would write it on the front of an index card like this:

> precipitation

On the back of the card, you would write the definition, like this:

> Falling products of condensation in the atmosphere, such as snow, rain, or hail.

Make one card for each vocabulary word. Then you can review the words. You can do this by yourself or with a friend or family member. If you are practicing by yourself, you can look at the word and try to recite the definition. Or, you can look at the definition, and try to guess the vocabulary word. Then, you can flip the card to see if you are correct. You could also have a friend or family member show you the card and tell you if you are correct.

LESSON #44

Using a Dictionary

Estimated Time: 15 minutes

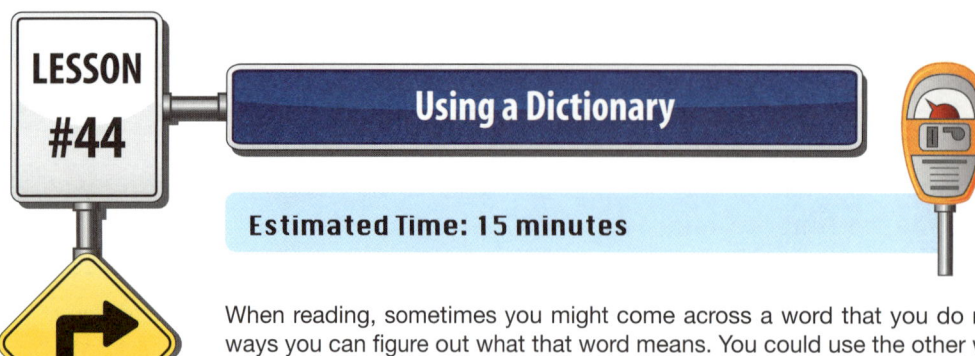

When reading, sometimes you might come across a word that you do not know. There are many ways you can figure out what that word means. You could use the other words around that word to help you figure out the meaning, you could ask another person what that word means, or you could use a dictionary. A *dictionary* is a book that contains words and their definitions, or meanings.

All of the words in a dictionary are arranged in alphabetical order to make it easier to find in the book. For example, if you want to look up the meaning of the word *surprise,* you would first turn to the section where all of the words start with the letter *s*. The second letter in *surprise* is *u,* so in the *s* section, go to where the *su* words are. Continue to look through the section until you find the entry for the word *surprise.* An *entry* is the word with its definition. Sometimes there is more than one definition for a word. You will also find the syllables, pronunciation, and part of speech for that particular word. The entry for *surprise* probably looks like this:

sur • prise (s∂r - ´prīz) noun
1 a. An attack made without warning. b. An act or an instance of coming upon something suddenly. 2. Something that surprises. 3. The state of being surprised.

sur • prise shows you how to break the word into syllables. The word surprise has two syllables.

s∂r - ´prīz tells you how to pronounce the word.

Noun is the part of speech of this word. Common parts of speech are noun, verb, adverb, adjective, and pronouns.

The next part of the entry is the definition or meaning of the word. As you can see, the word *surprise* has multiple meanings.

A dictionary is a very useful tool when you want to learn the meaning of a word, how to spell it, or find out other ways you can use the word.

Use a dictionary to answer the following questions:

What is one of the definitions of the word *exit?* _____
_____
_____

What part of speech is the word *door?* _____

DETOUR NEXT PAGE

END DETOUR

What is the plural form of the word *rabbit*? _____

Look up the word *basketball*. Write the word broken down into syllables.
_____

What is the definition of the word *alarm*? _____
_____
_____
_____

LESSON #45: Using a Thesaurus

Estimated Time: 15 minutes

In the last lesson, you used a dictionary to learn the definition of a word. Today, you will learn how to use a thesaurus. A *thesaurus* is a book, like a dictionary, but instead of giving you the meaning, it gives you synonyms and sometimes antonyms of a word. A *synonym* is a word that means the same, and an *antonym* is a word that means the opposite. For example, *large* and *big* are synonyms because they have a similar meaning. *Large* and *small* are antonyms because they are opposites. You might use a thesaurus when writing. In writing, you don't always want to use the same word. You might need another word that means the same thing or want a better way to say it. A thesaurus can help you with that.

Take the word *jump*. Imagine you are writing a paragraph about a rainy day, and you are describing what it was like to jump in puddles. You are getting tired of using the word *jump* over and over again. You can use a thesaurus to help you find a new word. You will look the word up just like you would in a dictionary. The words are arranged in alphabetical order, so go to the section with words beginning with *j*. Then, look for words beginning with *ju*, and continue looking down the page until you find the word *jump*.

The entry might look something like this:

> **jump**
> Synonyms: bound, hop, leap, spring, vault
> Related Words: bounce, lope, skip, caper, pounce, dive, pitch, plunge

DETOUR NEXT PAGE

END DETOUR

As you can see from the entry, there are five other words that are similar to the word *jump*. One of these words could be chosen to use in place of *jump* in your paragraph. This entry does not list any antonyms, or opposites. Some entries will list antonyms. The next time you need a new word, reach for your thesaurus!

Use a thesaurus to answer the following questions:

1. Name two synonyms of the word *thin*. _____

2. Name a synonym for the word *wave*. _____

3. Name a synonym for the word *jog*. _____

4. Find a new word to replace the underlined word in the sentence. This word should have a similar meaning to the underlined word.

   The kitten was <u>sleeping</u> on the couch. _____

5. Find a new word to replace the underlined word in the sentence. This word should have a similar meaning to the underlined word.

   The dog fetched the <u>stick</u>. _____

LESSON #46

Finding the Main Idea

Estimated Time: 15 minutes

This week, you will learn some strategies that can help you in language arts. In language arts, you learn about many things—reading, writing, spelling, and grammar. It can be difficult to keep it all straight!

Today's strategy is finding the main idea in a reading passage. The main idea is the most important thought of a paragraph or passage; it is the topic of the passage. Finding the main idea in a paragraph or reading passage helps you to remember the most important ideas of what you read.

To find the main idea in a passage, your first step is to read the passage. Sometimes the main idea is given in the title or sometimes in the first or last sentences. Other times, it takes the author until the middle of the paragraph to get to the main idea. You must read carefully in order to find the main idea. After you read, ask yourself: *What was this about?* Imagine you will tell your Guide a summary in about ten words. Your answer to this question will be the main idea. Once you figure out the main idea, you can highlight the sentence stating the main idea in the paragraph.

Let's look at an example of finding the main idea in a paragraph.

> As a girl, ==Carson spent a lot of time outdoors.== She collected the fossils of sea animals. She dug them from the bed of the Allegheny River. She learned about nature with her mother. They often went bird watching together. Carson ==loved to learn how different kinds of creatures lived.== Only one thing interested her more: writing.

Carefully read the paragraph. What is the main idea? What is the author trying to say? If you were going to give a short summary of this paragraph, what would you say? The main idea of this paragraph is that Rachel Carson spent a lot of time outside exploring animals in nature. Go back and underline or highlight the main idea. Combining two of the sentences in this paragraph will give you the main idea.

Read the following paragraph and write the main idea. If you want, you can underline or highlight the main idea in the paragraph.

> Rachel Carson began to write stories at a very young age. Her mother was very encouraging. Carson's first stories were about woodland animals. Her characters were birds and mice. After a few years, Carson published a story in *St. Nicholas*. It was the best-known children's magazine of the time. At the mere age of eleven, she had become a published writer!

LESSON #47: Finding Supporting Details in a Paragraph

Estimated Time: 15 minutes

In the previous lesson, you reviewed what a main idea is and how to find one in a paragraph. Many times when finding the main idea, you will also need to find supporting details. Supporting details are the ideas that describe the main idea. They help to make the point of the main idea stronger.

In order to find the supporting details, you will need to find the main idea first. Find the main idea and underline it with your pencil. After you locate the main idea, you will then want to think: *What in this paragraph helps describe the main idea?* Your answers to this question are the supporting details. Most paragraphs have two or three supporting details. Once you find them in the paragraph, highlight these details.

Take a look at this paragraph and how to find the supporting details. Read the following paragraph.

> Dr. Cooper's handheld mobile phone was a huge leap ahead. It still had some weaknesses, though. A person could only use it for a few phone calls at a time. The battery had to be charged for ten hours, but the user could only talk for thirty-five minutes. The phone only had three basic functions: dialing, listening, and talking. Still, this invention would soon help people be free to communicate from almost anywhere. By the 1990s, cell phones had become available and affordable to the average person. That is when the cell phone business began to take off.

What is the main idea of this paragraph? The main idea is Dr. Cooper's mobile phone was a huge leap ahead, but there were still some weaknesses. Underline these two sentences.

What are the details that help to describe the main idea? In this paragraph, there are three supporting details. Can you find them? They are: *the battery had to be charged for ten hours*, *the user could only talk for thirty-five minutes*, and *the phone only had three basic functions*. You will want to go back and highlight these three supporting details.

Practice finding the supporting details in the following paragraph. First read the paragraph. Then, identify the main idea. Underline it. Then, look for at least three supporting details. Write each detail on the lines below and highlight them in the paragraph.

> Cordless telephones are different than cell phones. A cordless phone has a base that is attached to a land line. The phone must be used within so many feet of its base or it will not work. A cell phone runs off a signal from a cell tower. Cell towers can be found all over the world. As you move, your call may switch from tower to tower without being dropped. That is how you have the freedom to talk almost anywhere while using a cell phone.

Supporting Details:

1. _____

2. _____

3. _____

LESSON #48

Vocabulary Activities

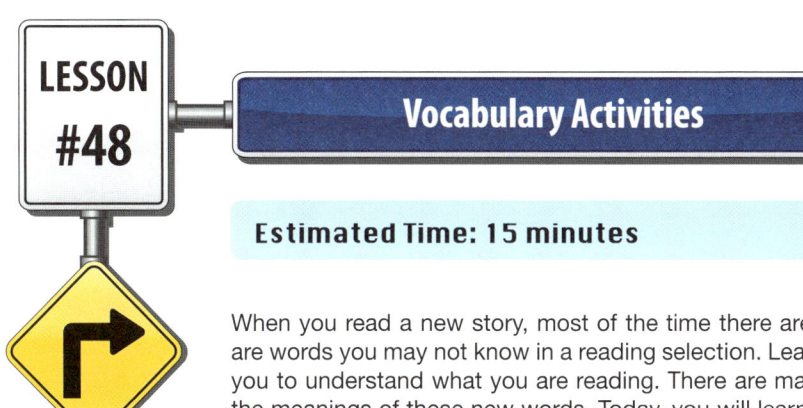

Estimated Time: 15 minutes

When you read a new story, most of the time there are new vocabulary words. *Vocabulary words* are words you may not know in a reading selection. Learning these words and what they mean help you to understand what you are reading. There are many different ways you can learn and review the meanings of these new words. Today, you will learn just one of these ways. You will need a list of vocabulary words from your reading story for this week, something to draw and color with, and index cards or a notebook.

Either on an index card or in your notebook, write the vocabulary word. If you are not sure of the meaning, you will need to look it up in a dictionary. Once you know the meaning of the word think of a picture you can draw to help you to remember the meaning of this word. Once you draw the picture, you can color it in.

For example, perhaps two of your vocabulary words this week are *sowed* and *tattered.* On an index card, or in a notebook, write the word. Then, draw a picture to help define the word and help you to remember what it means.

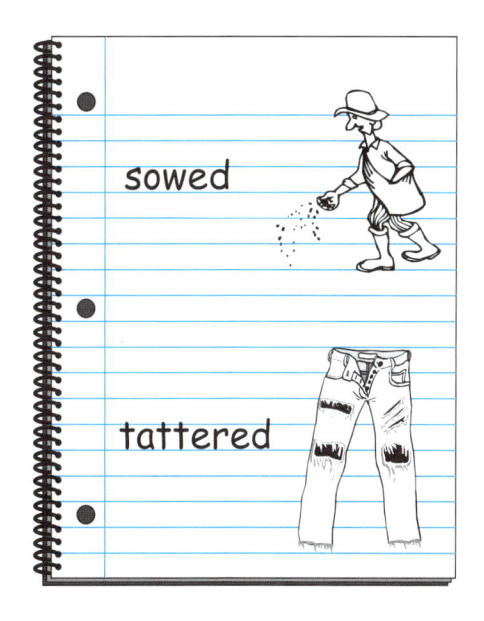

You can then quickly review the meanings of each word by flipping through your cards or notebook and looking at each of the pictures.

Use your vocabulary list for this week to make drawings for each vocabulary word. You can use this strategy anytime you are having trouble remembering the meaning of a word.

LESSON #49

Vocabulary Activities

Estimated Time: 15 minutes

You can use this activity to help you to review your vocabulary words before a quiz or test. Get a sheet of paper and fold it in half and in half again to make four boxes, like this:

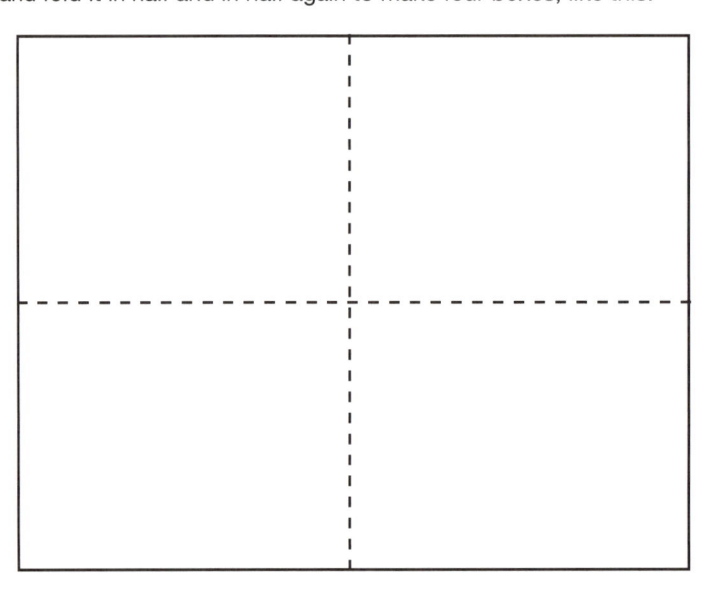

Then, draw a circle in the center of your paper, so it looks like this:

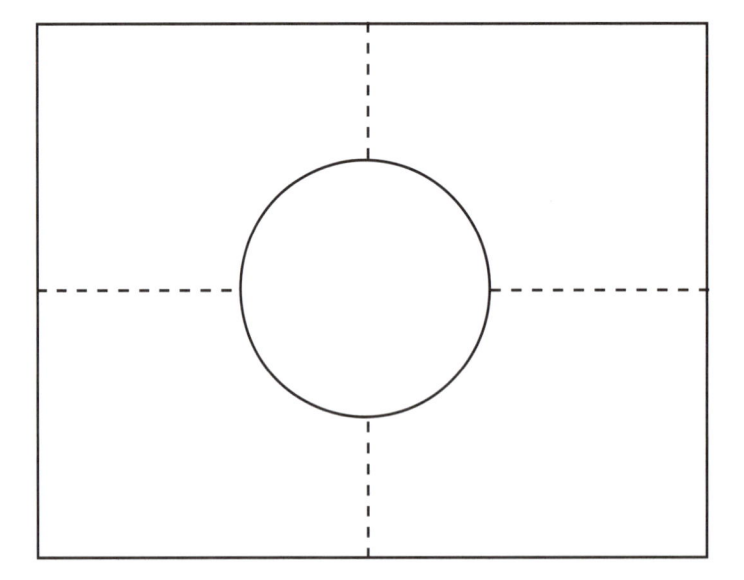

Write the vocabulary word in the circle. Perhaps one of the vocabulary words you want to review is *excited*. Write that word in the circle. In the upper left corner, write the definition of the word. In the upper right corner, use the word correctly in a sentence. In the lower left corner, write antonyms (opposites) of the word. In the lower right corner of the page, draw a picture to illustrate the word. If you can do all four of the activities correctly, then you know this word!

Try this activity using a vocabulary word of your choosing from this week.

LESSON #50

Spelling Activities

Estimated Time: 15 minutes

Each week, you probably have a list of spelling words to learn and memorize how to spell. You will want to learn the proper spelling of these words. Today, you will learn three different ways you can practice your spelling words. When studying for your next spelling test, try using one of these activities!

1. Borrow a cookie sheet from the kitchen (make sure to ask your Guide first). Sprinkle a thin layer of flour, sugar, or sand on the cookie sheet. Have your Guide tell you a word. Use your finger to write the word on the cookie sheet. Once you have properly spelled the word, gently shake the cookie sheet to erase the word. Continue one word at a time until you have reviewed your whole list!

2. Get a ball (any kind will do). Have your Guide say a word. Toss the ball back and forth. Each time a person tosses the ball, that person says the next letter in the word. For example, spell the word *cat*. You say *c*, and toss the ball to your Guide. Your Guide says *a* and tosses the ball back to you. You say *t* and toss the ball back to your Guide.

3. Spell your words using play dough. You will need a can or two of play dough. Have your Guide give you a word to spell. Make long snakes of play dough and form them into the letters in the word and then arrange them to correctly spell the word.

WEEK 11

LESSON #51: Math Strategies

Estimated Time: 10 minutes

This week, you will focus on some things you can do to help you solve math problems. Using manipulatives is one way that can help you solve math problems. A *manipulative* is something that you can use to represent a number. Use something small like pieces of cereal, small candies, or small blocks. For example, if you are given a problem like 2 + 3, you would count out 2 pieces of cereal and then 3 pieces of cereal. Sometimes seeing the number represented with objects can help you solve the problem a little easier.

Using manipulatives seems to work best when you are solving smaller math problems. It would be hard to use a small manipulative, like raisins, to solve the problem 163 + 78. That is because it would take quite some time to count out that many raisins! Not only would it take too much time but you may even have other difficulties, such as losing count.

The next time you are solving a math problem and need help, think about using manipulatives to help you find the answer.

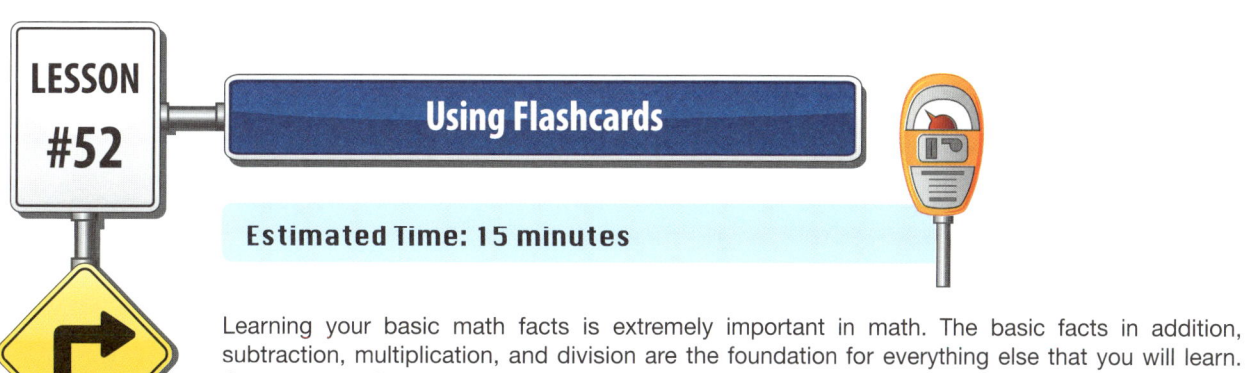

LESSON #52: Using Flashcards

Estimated Time: 15 minutes

Learning your basic math facts is extremely important in math. The basic facts in addition, subtraction, multiplication, and division are the foundation for everything else that you will learn. One way to help you learn your facts is to use flashcards every day. With your Guide, you should review the facts that you struggle with. Your goal is to know the answer to each fact automatically.

You can have your Guide show you each fact and you tell the answer. There are also many review games that you can play with flashcards. Here is one for you to try with your Guide.

Split the deck of flashcards in half. Keep one half and give your Guide the other half. Take turns showing each other a fact. If you get it right, you keep the card. If you get it wrong, you give it to the other player. Whichever player collects all of the cards first wins!

LESSON #53: Using Scratch Paper

Estimated Time: 15 minutes

One strategy that you may find helpful when taking a math test is to use scratch paper. On a test or even on a workbook page, there may not be enough space to solve the problem. Other times, the problem is written horizontally, and you might find it easier to solve it when it is written vertically. If this happens to you, get out a clean sheet of paper, carefully copy the numbers in the problem exactly, set it up right on the page, and then solve it on the piece of paper. Once you solve it on your scratch paper, make sure to transfer the correct answer to the test page so your Guide can check your work.

Get out a piece of paper. Copy these math problems onto your scratch paper and solve. If the problem is written horizontally, you can write it vertically to make it easier for you to solve. Once you have the answer, write it in the correct place.

1. 24 + 17 =
2. 68 − 21 =
3. 134 + 76 =

LESSON #54: Using Graphing Paper

Estimated Time: 15 minutes

In the last lesson, you learned how scratch paper can be helpful when solving a problem. Another strategy you can use is to use graph paper to help you line up the columns in a math problem. Let's look at how to use the graph paper to help you.

Take the problem 75 + 53 and write in on the graph paper. Write one digit in each box, making sure to line each column up correctly. Graph paper can help you to make sure the ones are in the correct column and the tens are in the correct column.

```
        7 5
      + 5 3
```

DETOUR NEXT PAGE

END DETOUR Now, you can solve as usual. This time, the columns are lined up properly helping eliminate any problems you may encounter.

```
    7 5
+   5 3
  1 2 8
```

If you have to carry, you will solve the problem exactly the same, except you will write the tens digit you are carrying above the tens column. See the example below.

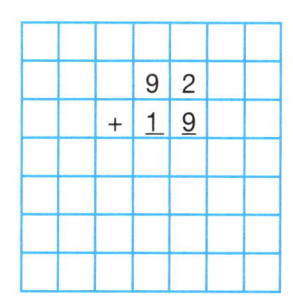

```
    9 2
+   1 9
```

Add in the ones column: 2 + 9 = 11. Write 1 in the ones column. Carry the other 1 to the tens column.

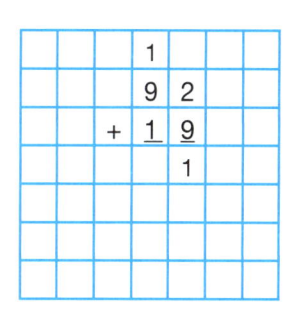

```
  1
    9 2
+   1 9
        1
```

Now add the tens column: 9 + 1 = 10 + 1 = 11. Write 1 in the tens column and the other 1 in the hundreds column.

Use a sheet of graph paper to help you solve the problems below.

1. 563 – 231   2. 634 + 73

```
  5 6 3
- 2 3 1
```

```
  6 3 4
+   7 3
```

LESSON #55

Using a Calculator

Estimated Time: 10 minutes

One tool that can be of help in math is a calculator. A calculator can be used to help you figure out a difficult problem. You should not use a calculator to help you solve basic facts. These you should have memorized. An example of a time when you should use a calculator is when you need to solve a problem quickly, such as finding out how much money you might need to have ten friends go bowling. If it costs $11 per person to bowl, you could get out your calculator and enter 10 x 11 to find out it will cost $110 total.

Take out your calculator. There are some basic things you will need to know about your calculator before you can begin using it. There will be a power button on your calculator. You must push this button to turn it on.

At first, the only keys you will need to use are the number keys, the operation keys (+, −, x, ÷), and the equal (=) key. The other part of your calculator you need to know is the display screen. This is where you will see the numbers you enter and the answer to your problem.

Take a few minutes today to play with your calculator. Practice pushing keys and see what happens. Next week, you will learn how to use your calculator to help you solve problems.

LESSON #56: Using a Calculator

Estimated Time: 15 minutes

Today, you will practice using a calculator. Remember, you should use a calculator when you need to solve a difficult problem. You should not use a calculator to solve a basic math fact. Get out your calculator, turn it on, and use it to help you solve the following math problem.

$$573 + 739$$

At this point in the year, you should already know how to solve a problem such as this one. If you needed to solve it quickly, you could use a calculator to help you find the sum.

To begin, make sure your calculator is on.

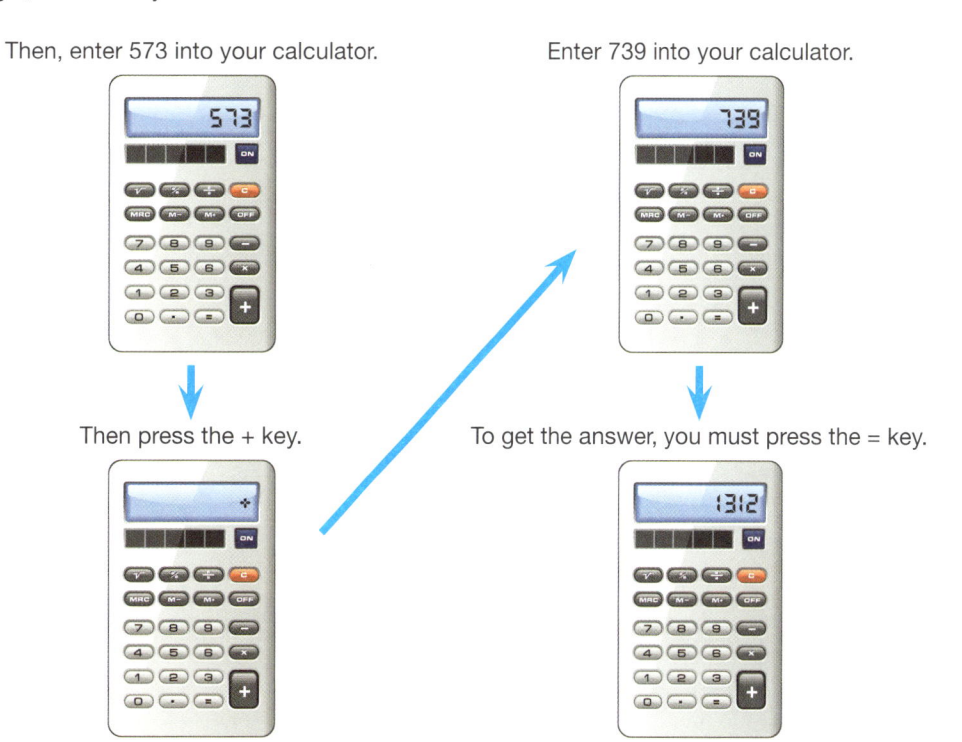

Then, enter 573 into your calculator.

Enter 739 into your calculator.

Then press the + key.

To get the answer, you must press the = key.

If you entered the number correctly, your calculator should be displaying 1,312 as the correct answer.

Make sure you are always careful entering numbers into a calculator. A calculator will always solve a problem correctly, but if you enter the wrong numbers, you will get a wrong answer!

Use your calculator to find the sums to the following problems:

1. 403 + 99 = _____

2. 398 + 831 = _____

3. 63 + 711 = _____

Lesson #57: Using a Calculator to Add

Estimated Time: 15 minutes

Yesterday, you practiced using a calculator to add two numbers. Sometimes you may need to add more than two numbers to get an answer. A calculator is a great tool to use to add many numbers. Don't forget to be very careful when entering numbers. If you enter the wrong number, you will get a wrong answer!

Use your calculator to find the answer to the following problem:

$$76 + 82 + 55$$

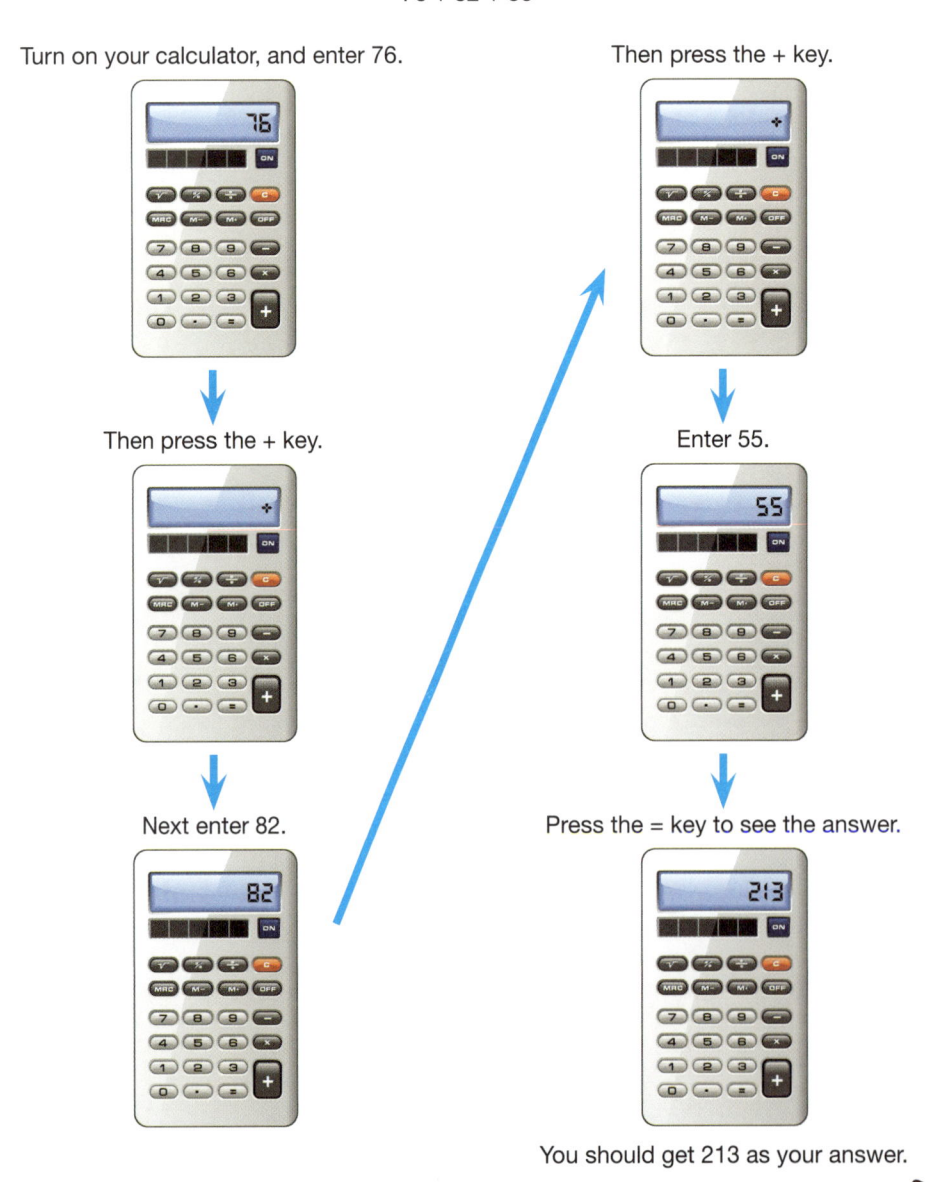

Turn on your calculator, and enter 76.

Then press the + key.

Next enter 82.

Then press the + key.

Enter 55.

Press the = key to see the answer.

You should get 213 as your answer.

DETOUR NEXT PAGE

END DETOUR

Use your calculator to solve the following problems:

1. 23 + 106 + 87 = _____

2. 71 + 13 + 31 = _____

3. 93 + 7 + 50 = _____

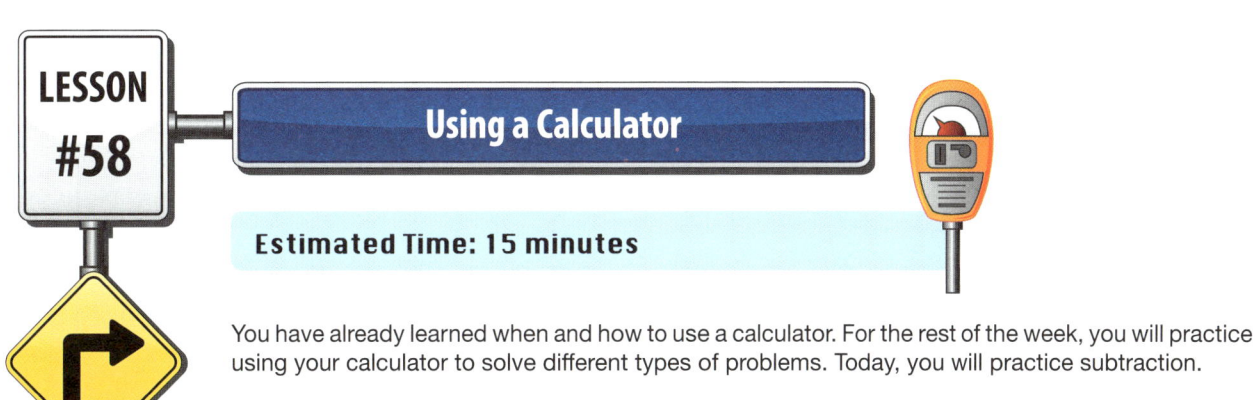

LESSON #58: Using a Calculator

Estimated Time: 15 minutes

You have already learned when and how to use a calculator. For the rest of the week, you will practice using your calculator to solve different types of problems. Today, you will practice subtraction.

Use your calculator to solve: 504 – 213.

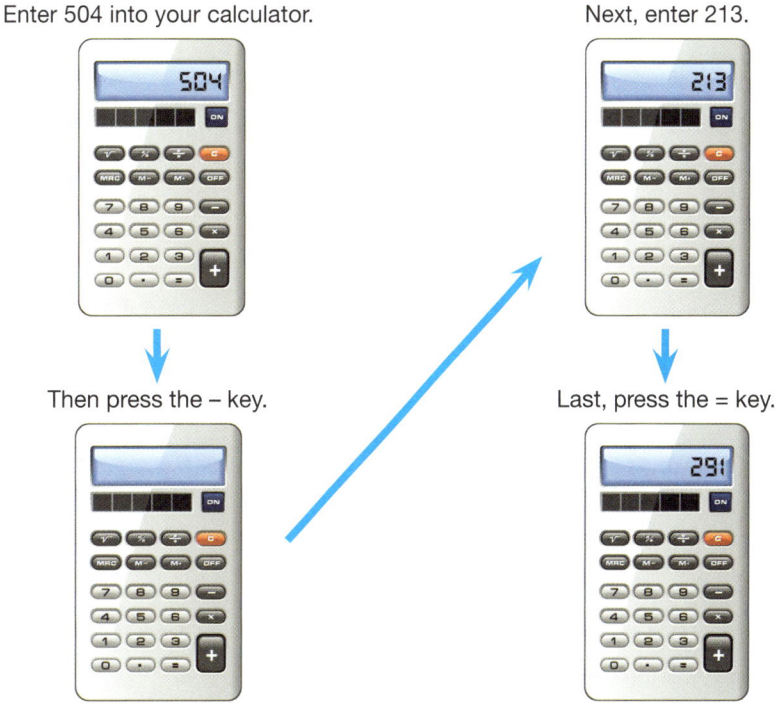

Enter 504 into your calculator.

Next, enter 213.

Then press the – key.

Last, press the = key.

Make sure you use the correct operation key. If you accidentally press +, you will get the wrong answer!

If you entered everything correctly into your calculator, you should get 291 as your answer.

Use your calculator to solve the following subtraction problems:

1. 87 – 32 = _____

2. 414 – 137 = _____

3. 999 – 456 = _____

LESSON #59

Using a Calculator to Multiply

Estimated Time: 15 minutes

So far this year, you have not practiced multiplication a lot. Later in the year you will learn and review multiplication facts. Even though you have not yet learned a lot about multiplication, you can still practice using your calculator to solve multiplication problems.

When you multiply, it is like adding over and over again. For example, 3 x 3 is like adding 3 + 3 + 3.

Use you calculator to find the product, or answer, to 11 x 11.

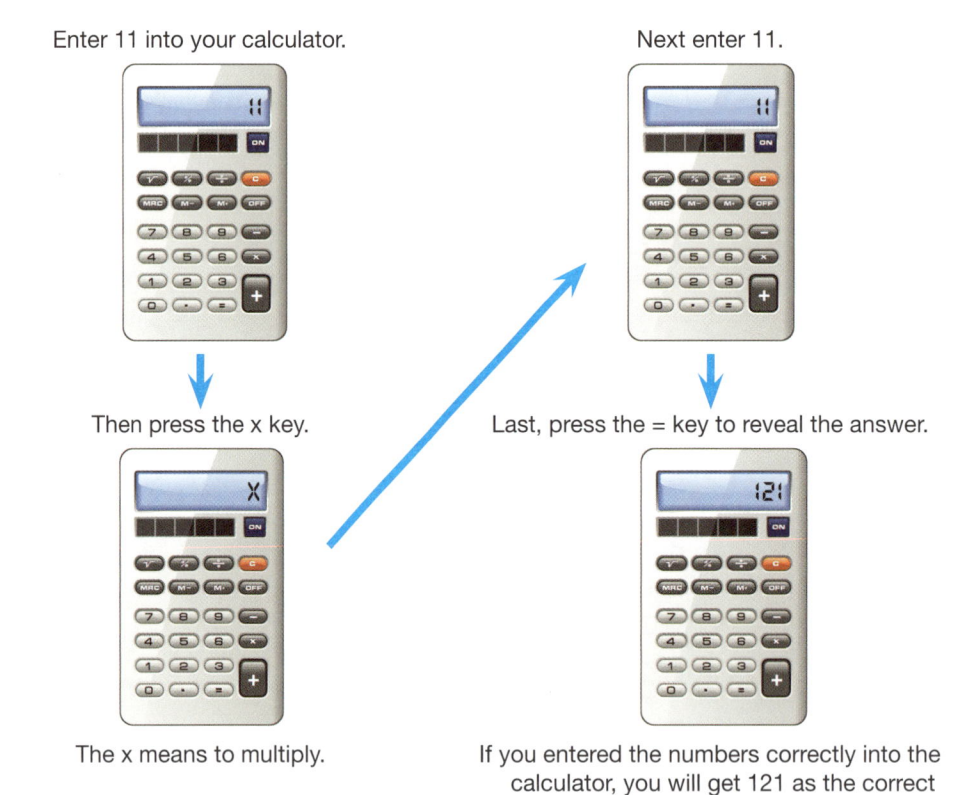

Enter 11 into your calculator.

Next enter 11.

Then press the x key.

Last, press the = key to reveal the answer.

The x means to multiply.

If you entered the numbers correctly into the calculator, you will get 121 as the correct answer.

Use your calculator to solve the following multiplication problems:

1. 15 x 9 = _____

2. 12 x 10 = _____

3. 14 x 8 = _____

LESSON #60

Using a Calculator to Divide

Estimated Time: 15 minutes

So far this year, you have not learned about division. Later in the year you will learn and review division facts. Even though you have not yet learned a lot about division, you can still practice using your calculator to solve these problems.

When you divide, it is like subtracting over and over again. For example, 10 ÷ 5 is like starting with 10 and subtracting 5 over and over until you get to 0.

Use you calculator to find the quotient, or answer, to 36 ÷ 4.

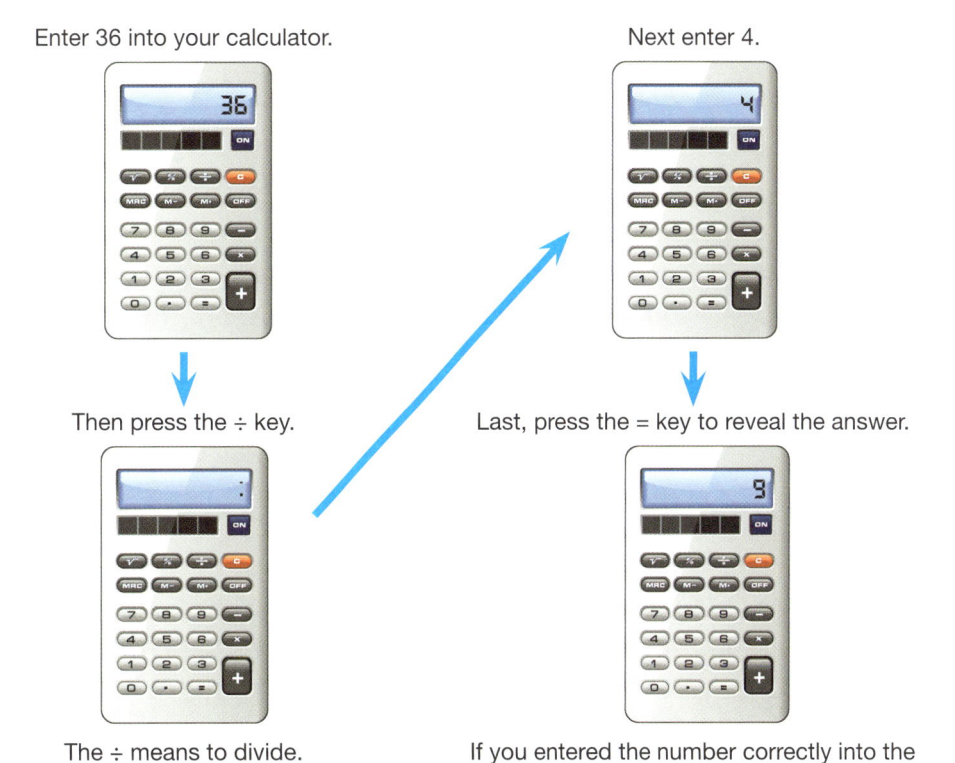

Enter 36 into your calculator.

Next enter 4.

Then press the ÷ key.

Last, press the = key to reveal the answer.

The ÷ means to divide.

If you entered the number correctly into the calculator, you will get 9 as the correct answer.

Use your calculator to solve the following division problems:

1. 88 ÷ 8 = _____

2. 54 ÷ 9 = _____

3. 100 ÷ 10 = _____

LESSON #61

Science Strategies

Estimated Time: 15 minutes

So far, you have learned different strategies to help you learn and review language arts and math. This week, you will learn different tips and strategies to help you review for science. The strategy you will learn about today is one that you have previously learned about. You have already learned about skimming your textbook before reading. This is a great way to prep your brain for learning.

When you skim the textbook, you are not reading in detail. You are looking at the headings, the pictures, and looking for key vocabulary words. This will give your brain an idea of what you will read. You can begin to think about what you already know about this topic. Then, when you are ready to read, you already have an idea of what you will learn about.

Lesson 3

How do we classify invertebrates?

Scientists have named more than a million species of invertebrates. That's a lot of animals that have no backbone!

Animals Without Backbones

Most of the animals on Earth do not have backbones. They are **invertebrates**. Some are too small to be seen with the naked eye. The largest invertebrates, which are giant squids, can easily stretch across the width of a basketball court. Some kinds of invertebrates include mollusks, worms, cnidarians, and arthropods.

Mollusks

A mollusk has a soft body without bones. This phylum includes animals such as snails, slugs, clams, and squids. Some mollusks, like clams, have a hard outer shell that protects them from being eaten. Some mollusks get oxygen by using gills. Others are able to absorb oxygen through their skin.

Worms

Worms belong to many different phyla. Flatworms are flat and very thin. They live in wet or damp places. Roundworms can live in water or on land. Segmented worms include the earthworm. Some kinds of worms are microscopic. Some are huge. One of the largest earthworms caught was about 7 meters (about 23 feet) long.

This strange-looking mollusk is a type of sea slug. It lives in tropical waters and eats algae.

END DETOUR

Skim the following paragraph from your science textbook.

> Newton's third law of motion explains that for every force, there is an equal and opposite force. This law of action and reaction explains how forces work together but on two different objects. A rocket taking off is a great example of Newton's third law of motion. The gases in the rocket burn and push in all directions. Some of the gases escape through the bottom of the rocket. This is the smoke that we observe at liftoff. This makes the force inside the rocket engine less in the back than it is in the front. The force pushes the rocket upward. Newton's discoveries made space travel possible.

Write one or two sentences telling what you think this paragraph will be about.

_____
_____
_____
_____

Before your next reading assignment in science, make sure to skim the assignment to help your brain get ready for reading.

LESSON #62 — Science Strategies

Estimated Time: 15 minutes

Another strategy to help you review science information is to have a discussion with your Guide. After you have read or completed lab work, discuss with your Guide what you learned. Talk about whether your experiment went the way you thought it would. If you got the result you expected talk about why this happened. If your hypothesis was wrong, talk about why you were wrong.

Talking about what you have learned helps you to keep this new information in your head.

You can use this list of questions to help guide your discussion with your Guide:

1. What are three things I learned in the reading assignment?
2. Did my experiment go as planned?
3. If yes, then why did it go as planned?
4. If no, why did the experiment go differently?
5. What would I still like to learn about this topic?

After your science lesson today, try talking to your Guide about what you just learned. You may be surprised at how much you have learned!

LESSON #63: Science Strategies

Estimated Time: 15 minutes

Did you know that asking questions is a good way to learn? When you ask questions and get answers to things you are curious about, you are learning! As you read in your science text, ask questions. You can either write your questions right in your science notebook, or you can write your questions on a sticky note. After you are finished reading or doing an experiment, try to find out the answers to your questions. You may find the answers by discussing with your Guide or researching your questions either in books or on reliable websites.

While you a completing your science lesson today, as you think of questions, jot down your questions. Then, try to find the answers. By finding the answers to your questions, you will find that you learn and understand the information even more.

LESSON #64: Science Strategies

Estimated Time: 15 minutes

Many times in science, you will have to memorize information. One way to help you memorize information is to use a mnemonic (ni - mon - ik) device. A mnemonic device is a pattern that helps you to remember things. Remembering things in a pattern helps your brain to recall, or think, of the information quickly.

There are many common mnemonic devices that people commonly use. For example, to help remember the order of the colors in a rainbow, the first letter of each color is turned into a man's name: Roy G. Biv. Each letter in the name stand for a color: red, orange, yellow, green, blue, indigo, violet. By remembering the name, it can help you to think of each of the colors in a rainbow.

If you are having difficulty remembering something, try to create a mnemonic device to help you remember.

Can you figure out what each of these mnemonic devices stand for? If you have thought about it, and just can't figure it out, try using an Internet search to figure out each of these mnemonic devices.

1. My Very Energetic Mother Just Served Us Nachos.
2. Every Good Boy Does Fine.
3. HOMES

LESSON #65

Science Strategies

Estimated Time: 15 minutes

Pictures are a powerful way to help you learn and remember information. Especially in science, pictures and diagrams are a great way for you to learn. After reading or doing an experiment, draw a picture or diagram in your science notebook to help you to remember what you just learned.

Here is an example of a diagram. Notice how this diagram shows the parts of the earth and each part is clearly labeled.

Earth's Interior

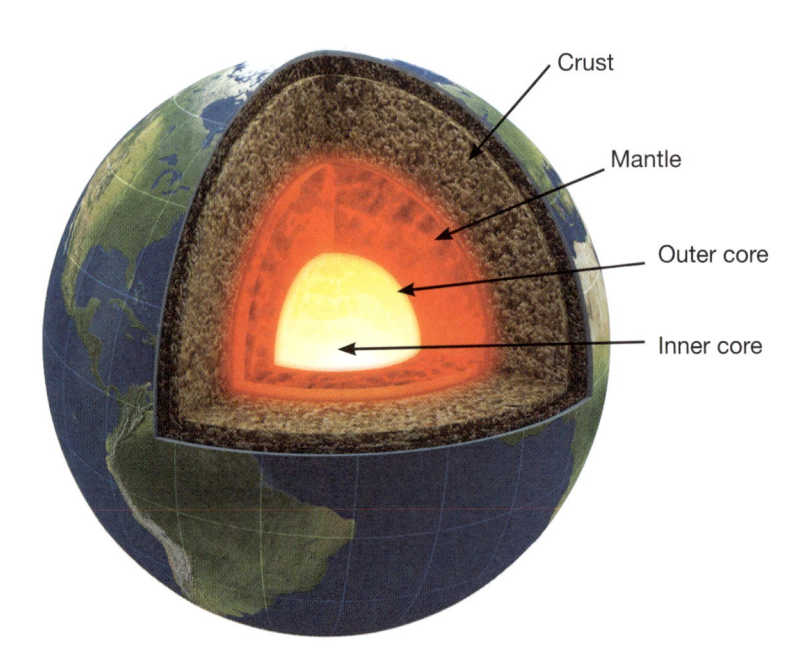

- Crust
- Mantle
- Outer core
- Inner core

Read the following paragraph and then draw a diagram to help you remember the information you read about.

A cycle is something that repeats. There are some cycles with which you are already familiar, but they are all very different. For one thing, the time it takes to complete different cycles varies tremendously. Let's take a look at some of these cycles. A laundry cycle may take an hour. The cycle of the seasons takes one year. A rock cycle is much longer. The *rock cycle* is the continuous changes of one kind of rock into another kind of rock. A rock cycle takes place over millions of years. You are going to see many cycles of laundry, but not even one cycle of a rock. However, over time, you can see the effects of the rock cycle. Look outside. The landscape is sculpted by the weathering and erosion that takes place. Places like canyons, caves, and mountain peaks can wear away after years of pollution and weather. You can see the results of a rock cycle around you. The rock cycle is not complete until the mineral goes through the cycle and returns to its original state.

DETOUR NEXT PAGE

END DETOUR → Now draw a diagram of the rock cycle:

If you are having trouble remembering a concept after reading or doing an experiment, draw a picture or diagram to help you remember and make it easy to review.

Social Studies Skills

Estimated Time: 15 minutes

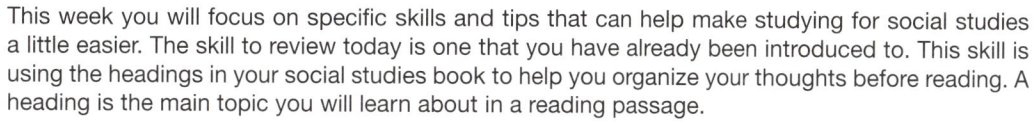

This week you will focus on specific skills and tips that can help make studying for social studies a little easier. The skill to review today is one that you have already been introduced to. This skill is using the headings in your social studies book to help you organize your thoughts before reading. A heading is the main topic you will learn about in a reading passage.

Let's look at an example of using headings to help you prepare to read. The headings are in bold before each section of text. Look at the headings only; you do not need to read the entire text.

Natural and Renewable Resources

Whether you have many or few natural resources available in your area, it is important to use them wisely. Some natural resources are renewable. A *renewable resource* is a resource that can be replaced. Trees and foods can be replanted. They are examples of renewable resources.

Other resources are nonrenewable. A *nonrenewable resource* is one that cannot be replaced. When these resources run out, there will not be anymore to use. Fuels such as oil and coal are examples of resources that are nonrenewable. We use these fuels to heat our homes, move our cars, and cook our food. Once we run out of oil and coal, we will have to find other sources of fuel.

For this reason, it is important to conserve our resources. To *conserve* means to use our resources carefully. There are three ways that we can conserve our resources. Remember three Rs: reduce, reuse, and recycle.

Reduce, Reuse, and Recycle

To *reduce* means to use less of a resource. When you brush your teeth, do you leave the water running? Water is a valuable resource. One way you can reduce the amount of water you use is to turn it off while you brush your teeth. You could also take shorter showers to use less water.

To *reuse* means to use something again. Instead of using plastic silverware that you throw away after each use, you can use real silverware that can be washed and used again.

To *recycle* also means to use a resource again, but when you recycle, you usually use a resource for something other than its original purpose. Trees are the natural resource used to make paper. Instead of throwing a newspaper away, you can recycle it as craft mats or gift wrap. You could use it as the liner in your hamster's cage.

END DETOUR → Think about the ways that you can reduce, reuse, and recycle.

What are the two headings in this section of reading? _____
_____

After seeing the two headings, what do you think you will be reading about? _____
_____
_____
_____

What do you already know about these topics? _____
_____
_____
_____

Now that you have thought about the headings, you are ready to read! Using these headings will help you to feel more comfortable about the information you are learning and help you to remember the new information.

LESSON #67

Social Studies Skills and Strategies

Estimated Time: 15 minutes

Many times in social studies, you learn about people, places, and dates. There will be times that you will need to remember the order in which certain events happened. One way to help you remember the order of events is to make a timeline. A *timeline* shows when things happened in the correct order. Timelines help to remember important dates and events in history in the correct order.

Perhaps you are getting ready for a big social studies test on the colonization of North America. You can review your notes and textbook, and as you are remembering events, you could create a timeline. It may look something like this:

DETOUR NEXT PAGE →

END DETOUR

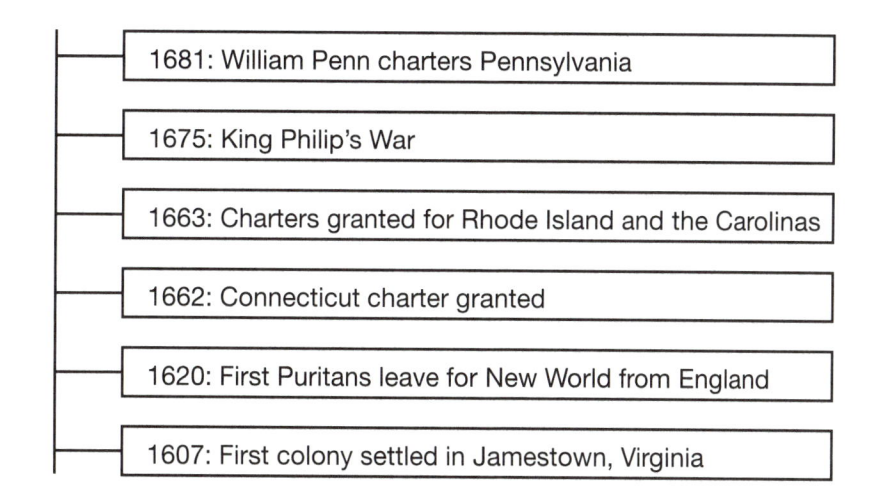

- 1681: William Penn charters Pennsylvania
- 1675: King Philip's War
- 1663: Charters granted for Rhode Island and the Carolinas
- 1662: Connecticut charter granted
- 1620: First Puritans leave for New World from England
- 1607: First colony settled in Jamestown, Virginia

As you can see, the earliest events are at the bottom of the timeline and the more recent events are at the top. You could even write each event in different colors to make it more interesting. As you create the timeline you are learning about the events and their order. After you are done creating the timeline, you can return back to it to review the order of events!

To help you practice making a timeline, use the space below to make a timeline of your life.

LESSON #68

Social Studies Skills and Strategies

Estimated Time: 15 minutes

Many of the ideas you learn about in social studies are about causes and effects. People in different parts of the world were looking for new land, which caused them to discover the New World. Another example of cause and effect in history is in colonial times. The colonists were not happy with the rules the King of England created. This caused the colonists to revolt and the Revolutionary War happened.

As you are reading and learning about history in your social studies textbook, you can make a cause and effect chart. On one side, you will write the cause, and on the other side, you will write what happened, or the effect.

Here is an example of a cause and effect chart. You may have already been introduced to Molly Pitcher in a previous social studies lesson. Reread the information about her below.

    Molly was born in New Jersey on October 13, 1754. Her real name was Mary Ludwig. As a young woman, she worked as a maid for a family in Carlisle, Pennsylvania. There she did jobs like cleaning, cooking, and laundry.

    When she was fifteen, she married John Hays. He was a barber in the town where she lived. Shortly after their marriage, John enlisted in the First Pennsylvania Artillery as a gunner. The Revolutionary War for America's freedom was just beginning. Mary traveled along with her husband and the other soldiers. She helped out around the camp by cooking, sewing, and doing laundry for the soldiers. She did all of these things as a volunteer, no one paid her or even asked her to do these jobs.

    Around the camp, the soldiers nicknamed her Molly. She got her other nickname one day during an important battle. On June 28, 1778 Molly's troops were fighting at the Battle of Monmouth. It was a very warm summer day and many of the soldiers were hot and thirsty. Molly found a small spring nearby. She filled up pitchers of water and carried them to the soldiers. She went right up to the front lines of the battle to give the soldiers water! They started calling her Molly Pitcher for the many pitchers of water she carried that day.

    Molly's husband, John, got wounded during battle. Even though Molly was not trained to fight in the army, she knew John's job well enough to help. She picked up the rammer and kept the cannon firing.

    Another soldier, named Joseph Martin, witnessed Molly Pitcher in action. He told people that he saw a cannonball shot by their enemies go right between her legs! Instead of running away or getting scared, she simply said it was a good thing the cannon didn't hit any higher. She kept on fighting at the cannon for the rest of the battle! The American army ended up winning the battle with Molly's help!

    As more people started to hear about Molly Pitcher's story, she became an army heroine. A heroine is a girl or woman who is admired for her great and noble acts. To honor her, the state of Pennsylvania started giving her $40 a year for her brave work. It may not sound like much money, but it is the equivalent to over $2,400 today! Molly Pitcher was a brave volunteer who helped her community by taking care of the soldiers and fighting along with them.

DETOUR NEXT PAGE

END DETOUR Now, that you have read about Molly Pitcher, take a look at an example of the cause and effect chart about her life. When an event happens, it causes an effect.

Cause	Effect
Molly's husband was a soldier in the Revolutionary War.	Molly traveled around with the soldiers and helped them.
Molly brought pitchers of water on hot summer days to the thirsty soldiers.	The soldiers nicknamed her "Molly Pitcher."
Molly's husband, John, was wounded in battle.	Molly kept firing the cannon.
Molly kept fighting in the battle.	The American army won the battle.
Molly was brave in helping her country.	Pennsylvania gave her $40 a year for her brave work.

Writing the information in a notebook with the causes and effects of certain events in history can help you to remember more about the event. Then, after you have filled in the information in the chart, you can then go back and easily review what you have written.

After you read your social studies textbook today, make a cause and effect chart of the information you learned.

LESSON #69

Social Studies Skills and Strategies

Estimated Time: 15 minutes

As you have already learned in many of these activities, reading words and seeing pictures is a very powerful way to learn and remember information. One way to help you remember what you have read in your social studies text is to draw a picture of it. Use what you have read and learned and imagine it in your head. Put your thoughts into a picture. It does not have to be a perfectly drawn picture; you can even make stick figures if you need to! Your picture should show all of the main ideas of what you have read.

Read the following paragraphs:

> Police officers always wear a uniform when they are on duty. Their uniforms have a few key parts that help make their job easier. One of them is a radio that is attached so they can talk to other officers and call for help. They also have tools used to handle crowds or criminals, like a gun or a crowbar. Officers also have a badge to let the public know that they are an official member of the police force.
>
> Police officers are people that you can trust. If you are ever lost, a police officer can help you find your way. If you are ever hurt or need help, a police officer will get you the assistance you need. You will see officers all around the community since they do so many different things as a service to the public.

DETOUR NEXT PAGE

END DETOUR Draw a picture of what you just read.

LESSON #70

Social Studies Skills and Strategies

Estimated Time: 15 minutes

The last strategy you will learn that can help you get ready for a test is to make up a quiz. You can do this many different ways, but one good way to do this is to work with your Guide. Look over the information in your textbook that you know will be covered on the test. Ask your Guide to help you think about the information that may be covered on the upcoming test. From the textbook, make up test questions. Then, have your Guide either ask you the questions and you can tell your Guide the answer, or you can have your Guide give you the questions and you can write your answers. Either way, it will make for a great review before a test!

Read the following paragraph. Make at least two possible test questions from the information you read.

A *rural community* is one where the towns are small and far apart. People often describe this as the countryside. You will usually see open fields and farms in a rural community. Many people live and work on farms. Houses are spread far apart and often have large yards and sometimes even wooded areas around them.

Make up two test questions based on what you just read.

_____
_____
_____
_____

Lesson #71: Outlines

Estimated Time: 15 minutes

This week you will practice a skill that can be a very valuable study tool. You will learn how to create an outline. An outline is a way to find and organize the main ideas and supporting details from something you have read. An outline is almost like a skeleton; it gives the main structure of your textbook by telling only the main details.

Let's look at an example of an outline. This outline is based on the paragraphs below. Read the outline and then read the text to see how the outline was created.

I. The Constitution of the United States

    A. Is a document that outlines the rules and law of the United States of America.

    B. Is the highest law in the United States.

II. Citizenship

    A. A person is a citizen of the United States if he or she is born here.

    B. A citizen of the United States is protected by the country and has all the rights and responsibilities that a citizen has.

    C. A person not born in the United States can become a citizen if they follow certain rules.

This outline was done on a lesson from social studies, but outlining can be used in any subject to help review and remember before a test. The main idea of a paragraph is noted by using a Roman numeral (I, II, III). The supporting details of a paragraph are shown using uppercase letters (A, B, C). When making an outline, you should find the main idea of a paragraph and then give the most important supporting details. You can then use the outline you created to study from.

In the remaining lessons this week, you will create an outline from a textbook.

    When the United States became a free country, the forefathers of our nation drafted our Constitution. The Constitution is a document that outlines the rules and laws of our country. It also tells how our government is to be run. The Constitution is the highest law; everything in it must be followed in the United States.

    Citizenship is a topic in the Constitution. It defines citizenship as, "All persons born or naturalized in the United States, and subject to the jurisdiction thereof, are citizens of the United States and of the State wherein they reside." This means that the United States only claims a person as a citizen if they have met one of the ways to become a citizen.

    The standard and easiest way to become a citizen is to simply be born in the United States. If you were born in any of the fifty states, then you are already a citizen. This means you are under protection by the United States and you have all the rights and responsibilities of a citizen. Ask your Guide where you were born and if you are a US citizen.

DETOUR NEXT PAGE

END DETOUR

If a person was not born in the United States, there are still some other ways that he can become a citizen of the country. The first is by going through the naturalization process. A person must apply for citizenship and meet the requirements below.

- Must be at least eighteen years old.
- Must have lived in one state for three months.
- Must have been living in the United States for at least three years.
- Must be able to speak, read, and write in English.
- Must have good moral character.
- Must take the oath of allegiance to America.

Another way for a person to become a citizen is to get a derivative or acquired citizenship. These processes are for children under eighteen years old. When a child's parent becomes a citizen through the naturalization process, the child becomes a derivative citizen. If a child is born outside of the United States but has at least one parent who is a United States citizen, then the child is an acquired citizen.

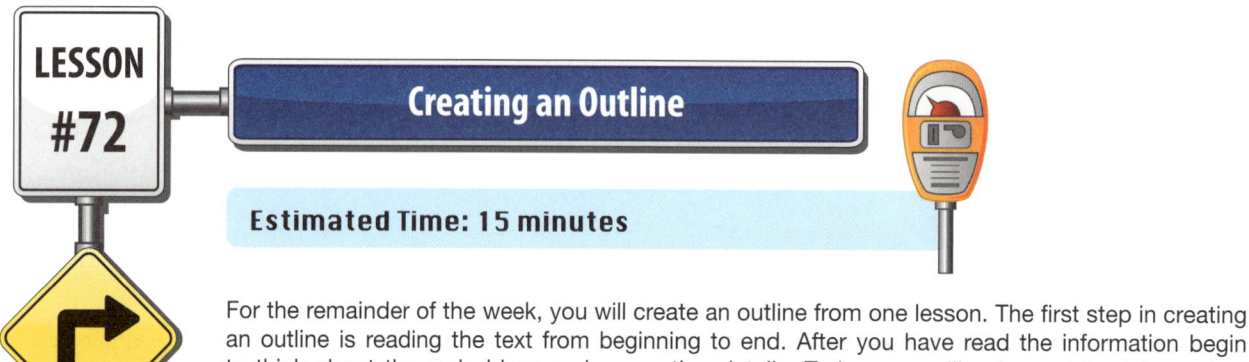

Lesson #72: Creating an Outline

Estimated Time: 15 minutes

For the remainder of the week, you will create an outline from one lesson. The first step in creating an outline is reading the text from beginning to end. After you have read the information begin to think about the main ideas and supporting details. Today, you will only read the information. Tomorrow, you will begin to write the outline.

Read the following information in preparation to writing an outline.

Rain, snow, sleet, and hail occur often. When precipitation falls from the sky, it flows over the land into streams and other bodies of water. Some evaporates, and some seeps into the ground.

Water that flows over the surface of the earth contributes to the weathering or the erosion of land. *Weathering* is the process that breaks down rocks into various materials, including soil. Weathering can occur due to weather, animals, or plants. *Erosion* is the wearing away and the movement of these weathered materials from one place to another.

There are two types of weathering. One type is mechanical weathering. *Mechanical weathering* is when rocks are broken into smaller rocks. It happens when rocks come into contact with another object. This can happen when rocks are next to each other. The rocks will rub against each other, small particles of the rock will break off, and over time the rock will change. Mechanical weathering can also occur when ice rubs against a rock and wears away bits if it. Sometimes plants grow through a rock breaking it apart, which is another form of mechanical weathering. Also, water runs through holes in rocks. When temperatures change, the water may freeze and thaw causing the rock to eventually break apart.

DETOUR NEXT PAGE

END DETOUR

The other type of weathering is chemical weathering. This happens when rocks are weathered by a chemical reaction. One chemical reaction that causes rocks to change is oxidation. Hydration, or the combining of rocks with water, can cause them to turn to clay. Clay is much softer and can be broken apart easily. Carbonation is caused when carbonic acid reacts with minerals in a rock causing it to break down. Typically a physical change happens in a dry, cold environment and a chemical change will occur in a moist, hot environment.

Here are some factors that cause weathering and erosion.
a. wind
b. water
c. glaciers
d. waves

Weathering and erosion work together to change the environment. Weathering, either mechanical or chemical, changes the environment and then erosion carries the sediments, or the particles, away. Weathering takes place over a period of time. The harder the rock, the longer it will take to weather.

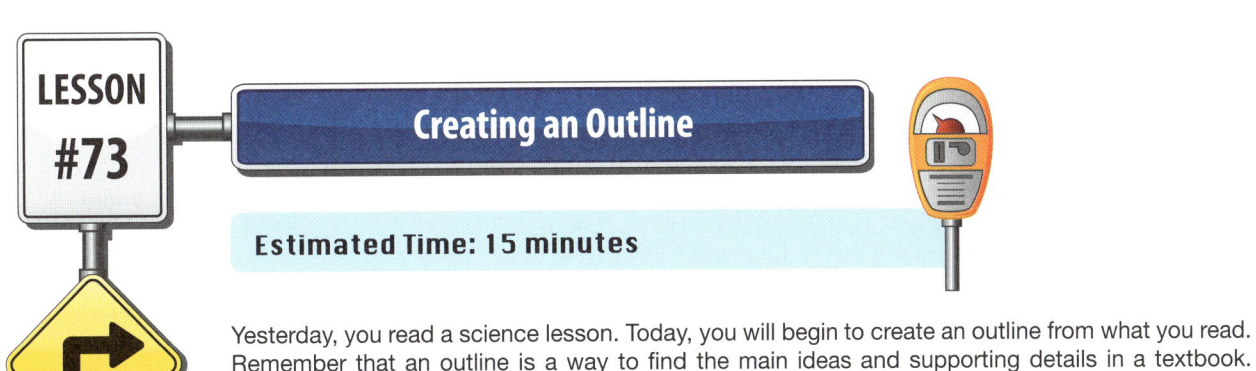

LESSON #73: Creating an Outline

Estimated Time: 15 minutes

Yesterday, you read a science lesson. Today, you will begin to create an outline from what you read. Remember that an outline is a way to find the main ideas and supporting details in a textbook. Today, you will begin to make the outline from just the first two paragraphs. Think of a main idea for these two paragraphs. Write it next to the Roman number I below. Then, find at least two supporting details. Write one supporting detail next to the uppercase letter A and the other next to the uppercase letter B. If you can find one more supporting detail, write C under B and write your last detail.

Rain, snow, sleet, and hail occur often. When precipitation falls from the sky, it flows over the land into streams and other bodies of water. Some evaporates, and some seeps into the ground.

Water that flows over the surface of the earth contributes to the weathering or the erosion of land. *Weathering* is the process that breaks down rocks into various materials, including soil. Weathering can occur due to weather, animals, or plants. *Erosion* is the wearing away and the movement of these weathered materials from one place to another.

I. _____
   A. _____
      _____
   B. _____
      _____

LESSON #74

Creating an Outline

Estimated Time: 15 minutes

Today, you will continue to create an outline. Reread the paragraphs below. In these two paragraphs, there are two main ideas. Write one each next to the Roman numbers II and III below. Then, find at least two supporting details for each main idea. Write the one supporting detail next to the uppercase letter A and write the other next to the uppercase letter B. If you can find one more supporting detail, write C under B and write your last detail.

There are two types of weathering. One type is mechanical weathering. *Mechanical weathering* is when rocks are broken into smaller rocks. It happens when rocks come into contact with another object. This can happen when rocks are next to each other. The rocks will rub against each other, small particles of the rock will break off, and over time the rock will change. Mechanical weathering can also occur when ice rubs against a rock and wears away bits of it. Sometimes plants grow through a rock breaking it apart, which is another form of mechanical weathering. Also, water runs through holes in rocks. When temperatures change, the water may freeze and thaw, causing the rock to eventually break apart.

The other type of weathering is chemical weathering. This happens when rocks are weathered by a chemical reaction. One chemical reaction that causes rocks to change is oxidation. Hydration, or the combining of rocks with water, can cause them to turn to clay. Clay is much softer and can be broken apart easily. Carbonation is caused when carbonic acid reacts with minerals in a rock causing it to break down. Typically a physical change happens in a dry, cold environment and a chemical change will occur in a moist, hot environment.

Here are some factors that cause weathering and erosion.
a. wind
b. water
c. glaciers
d. waves

II. _____
   A. _____
   B. _____

III. _____
   A. _____
   B. _____

LESSON #75

Creating an Outline

Estimated Time: 15 minutes

Today, you will complete the outline you have been working on for the past two days. Reread the paragraph below. In this paragraph, there is just one main idea. Write it next to the Roman numeral IV. Then, find at least two supporting details for the main idea. Write one supporting detail next to the uppercase letter A and the other next to the uppercase letter B. If you can find one more supporting detail, write C under B and write your last detail.

> Weathering and erosion work together to change the environment. Weathering, either mechanical or chemical, changes the environment and then erosion carries the sediments, or the particles, away. Weathering takes place over a period of time. The harder the rock, the longer it will take to weather.

IV. _____
   A. _____
      _____
   B. _____
      _____

WEEK 16

LESSON #76 — Tests

Estimated Time: 10 minutes

Tests are always a part of school and learning. Tests show your teacher or your Guide what you have learned. There are many different types of tests that you take throughout your schooling. You may be used to taking spelling tests, vocabulary, and math tests. This year you will be introduced to a few more types of tests like essay tests and standardized tests. Throughout this week you will learn about these different types of tests and why you need to take them.

Why is taking tests important? _____
_____
_____

LESSON #77 — Short Quiz

Estimated Time: 15 minutes

One type of test you have already taken this year, and will continue to take, is the short quiz. This type of test may include spelling tests, vocabulary tests, or quick tests of math facts. These types of quizzes are given frequently for you to show what you know quickly.

These types of quizzes are easy to prepare for and they do not take a long time to complete. You have already learned a few techniques to help you study for spelling tests and vocabulary tests. If you are taking a timed test in math on multiplication facts, you will want to prepare for this type of test by quickly practicing flashcards.

Name three kinds of short quizzes you may take:
_____
_____
_____

How can you prepare for these types of tests? _____
_____
_____

LESSON #78

Tests: End of Unit Tests

Estimated Time: 15 minutes

Another type of test that you will take this year is an end of the unit test. This is a much bigger test than a spelling or math fact quiz. An end of the unit test will ask you questions about everything you have learned in a unit on *Charlotte's Web*, for example. You may be expected to tell the meaning of vocabulary words, remember the details of the story, and answer questions about reading skills such as cause and effect. These types of tests are fairly long and will require you to take your time to make sure you get as many questions correct as possible.

On these tests, you may see more than one type of question. Common types of questions can be matching, true or false, multiple choice, or essay tests. Later in this book, you will learn strategies to help you learn how to answer these types of questions.

To prepare for these types of tests, you will want to use one of the many study strategies you have already been introduced to. Review strategies such as outlining, making a timeline, having a discussion with your Guide, rereading for understanding, and reviewing notes you have taken will all help you to prepare for these larger and very important tests.

Why are end of the unit tests important? _____

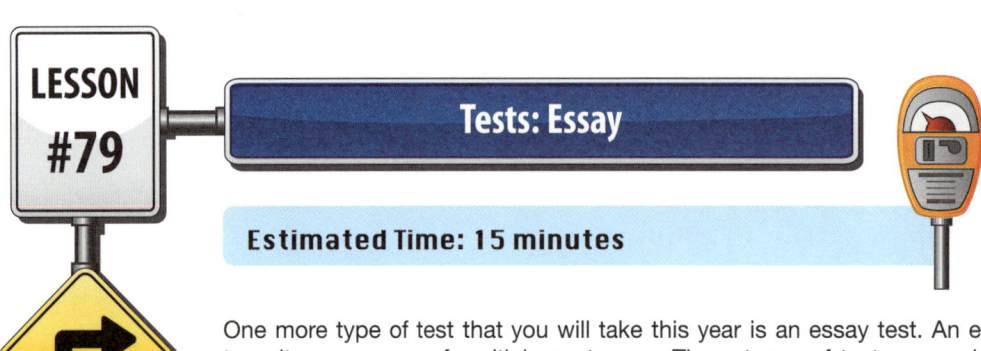

_____

LESSON #79

Tests: Essay

Estimated Time: 15 minutes

One more type of test that you will take this year is an essay test. An essay test will require you to write an answer of multiple sentences. These types of test are made for you to explain your thoughts to make sure you understood the material you were supposed to learn. You will have essay questions to answer in every subject, even math! Even in math, it is important for you to explain how you found your answer.

Here is an example of an essay question you might see on a science test:

Explain why landslides happen. Name two common locations that landslides can take place.

Here is an example of a good essay answer:

Landslides happen when loose soil and rocks slide down a large hill or mountain. Heavy rain or snow can also trigger dirt and rocks to slide down causing a landslide. Two common locations that landslides can occur are on large hills or mountains without a lot of trees or plants.

DETOUR NEXT PAGE

END DETOUR

Notice that this answer completely answers the question that was asked. The question asked two things, and the answer gave two answers. The answer is also written in complete sentences. An essay answer must be written in a complete sentence. One or two word answers are not acceptable. After you have written your answer, go back and reread the question. Then, look in your answer to make sure you have fully answered what you were asked.

Name two things you must do in an answer to an essay question.

1. _____
   _____
   _____

2. _____
   _____
   _____

LESSON #80: Tests: Standardized Tests

Estimated Time: 15 minutes

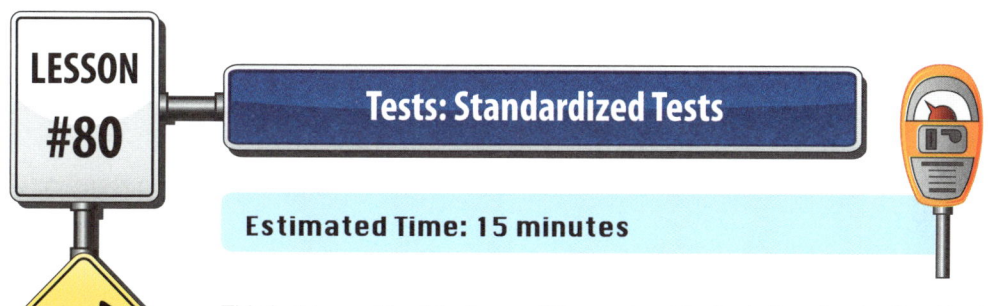

This last type of test that you will learn about today is the standardized test. These tests are typically not given a grade like unit tests or quizzes. Standardized tests are usually given to see if you have learned what you were supposed to learn during the school year. Every state in the United States has its own standardized test that is given each year. In Pennsylvania, the PSSA, or Pennsylvania System of School Assessment, is given to most students. Students in Virginia take a similar test called Standards of Learning, and kids in Texas take the TAKS, or Texas Assessment of Knowledge of Skills, every year. These tests are designed to show parents, schools, and the government that your school is doing what they are supposed to do to educate you.

These types of tests usually have a combination of multiple choice and essay questions. Preparing for these tests usually take some time. You begin to prepare for them on the first day of school. You will be asked questions about things you learn all school year long.

Next week, you will learn more about what a standardized test may look like, and how you can prepare for one.

Why do students have to take standardized tests? _____
_____
_____
_____

LESSON #81: Standardized Testing

Estimated Time: 15 minutes

Last week, you learned about different types of tests, and one of those tests was the standardized test. These big tests are something new to you this school year. This week, you will learn about some of the things you will need to do for these special tests.

The main difference between this test and others that you may take is that you will not earn a letter grade on this test. It does not count as a grade toward any subject. You may earn a score such as "proficient," which tells your teachers and Guide that you have learned what you were supposed to this school year.

Another big difference is that this test will be almost all multiple choice questions. A *multiple choice question* asks a question and gives you at least three choices for an answer, and you must choose one of them. Many times standardized tests also have special essay questions in math and reading. You may also have to answer questions about grammar, science, or social studies.

Later this week, you will learn about a few more differences between these standardized tests and the tests you may take with your Guide.

List at least two differences between standardized tests and other tests that you are used to.

1. _____
   _____

2. _____
   _____

LESSON #82: Getting Ready for Standardized Tests

Estimated Time: 15 minutes

Getting ready for a standardized test is a little different than preparing for a quiz or unit test. This is not a test that you can study for the way you can study for a unit test. By completing your daily lessons, you will be ready and prepared for these very important tests.

You may be taking the test in a traditional school setting, or maybe in a different location or setting. To get ready to take the test, you will need to have all of the materials you need in front of you. You will need to make sure to have a few pencils, a pencil sharpener, a highlighter, and a calculator. These are the most important school tools that you will need to do your best on the test.

What are some things you will need to take a standardized test?
_____
_____

LESSON #83

Taking a Standardized Test

Estimated Time: 15 minutes

On the day you take a standardized test, the first thing you will need to do is write your name on the test. However, it is not just a blank line for you to write your name. Because these tests are usually graded by a computer, you will have to write your name in a very specific way.

Below is a sample of one way you may be asked to write your name. In the first section, you will write your last name, with one letter in each box. In the second section, you will write your full first name, again with one letter in each box. Then, you will have to color in the circle that has the correct letter to match the letter in the box. If you do this incorrectly, the computer grading your test may spell your name incorrectly!

Last Name: ANDERSON

First Name: MARISA

Now that you have seen an example of the correct way to write your name on a test, practice writing your name on the test booklet cover and color in the correct circle for each letter.

Last Name   First Name

LESSON #84

Answering Test Questions

Estimated Time: 15 minutes

On standardized tests, when you are asked a question, you will be given three or four answers to choose from. Rather than writing the answer in the test, you will fill in a circle next to the answer you choose. See the example below.

Which is an opinion?

○ My dog is brown.

● My dog is the best dog.

○ My dog likes toys.

To show the answer you think is correct, you will color in the circle next to your choice. You have to color the circle in completely. You cannot put an x in the circle; you cannot circle your answer. You must completely fill in the circle as neatly as possible.

These types of questions are graded by a computer. If you do not fill in the answer circle correctly, your answer could be marked wrong.

Answer the questions below, and practice coloring in the correct answer circle.

1. 3 + 6 =

   ○ 12

   ○ 3

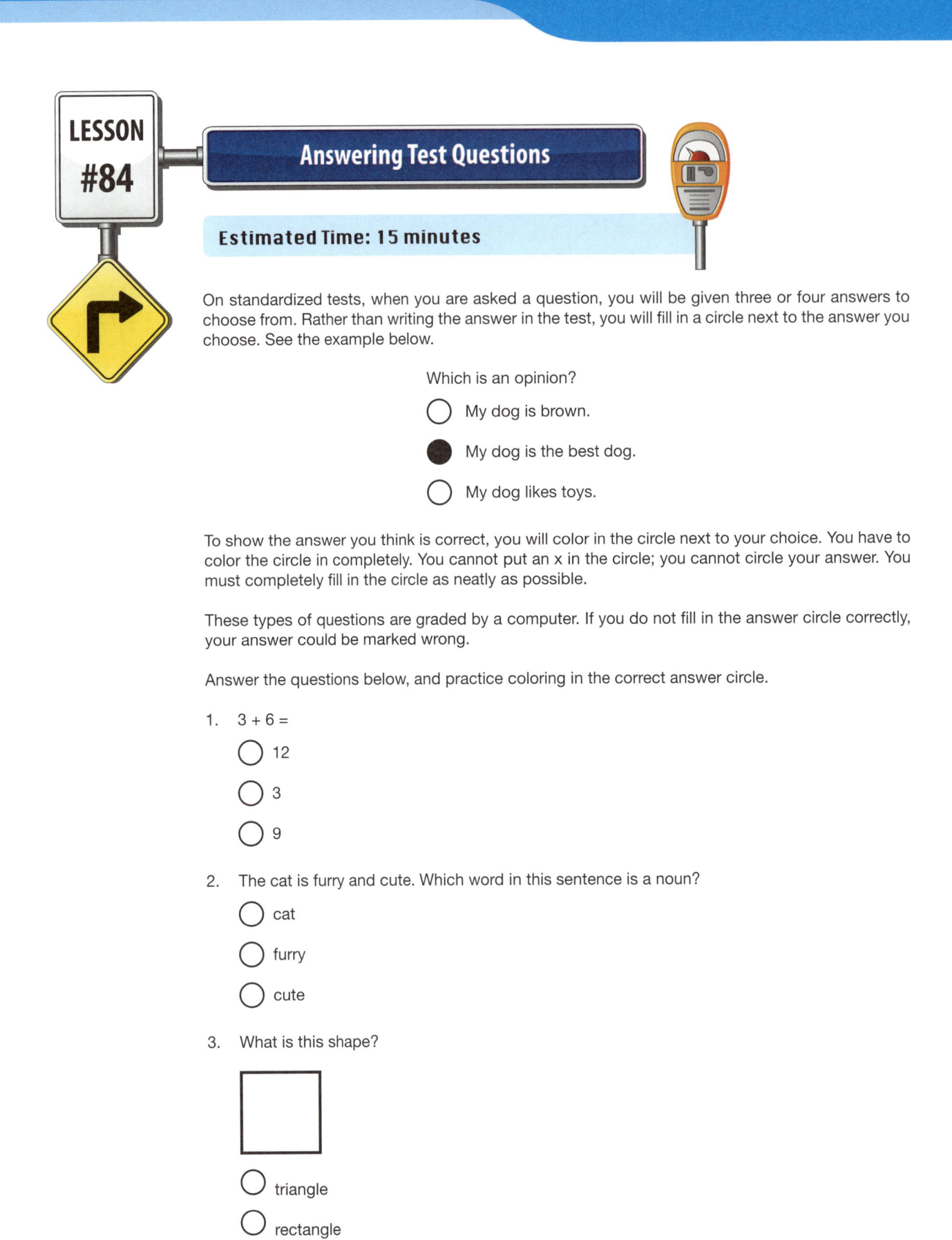

   ○ 9

2. The cat is furry and cute. Which word in this sentence is a noun?

   ○ cat

   ○ furry

   ○ cute

3. What is this shape?

   ○ triangle

   ○ rectangle

   ○ square

LESSON #85

Answering an Essay Question

Estimated Time: 15 minutes

When answering an essay question or an open-ended question, you have to be very careful about where to write your answer. In order to properly score, or grade your test, you have to write your answer within a special box, sometimes called a response box. This is so the person grading your test knows exactly where your answer is.

Let's look at an example.

Give a short description of the character of Wilbur at the beginning of *Charlotte's Web*.

Wilbur is one of the characters in the novel Charlotte's Web. Wilbur is a pig. He was the runt of the litter, but was saved by a little girl named Fern. Wilbur was eventually sent to Zuckerman's farm to live. He is an extraordinary pig, according to his spider friend, Charlotte.
_____
_____
_____

Notice how the student's response is written inside the box. None of the words extend beyond the lines of the box. It is important to keep your answer on the lines, inside the box, and written as neatly as possible.

Practice writing an answer to a question within a response box.

Write a short paragraph about your family.
_____
_____
_____
_____
_____
_____

LESSON #86: Preparing for a Test

Estimated Time: 15 minutes

So far this year, you have learned many strategies to help you keep track of your time, take notes, and study for tests. Last week, you learned about standardized tests and some of the differences between a quiz or test and a standardized test. This week, you will review some of the strategies and tips you have already learned to help you prepare for tests.

One of the first things you will need to know when preparing for a test is when the test will be given. Talk with your Guide every couple of days to ask when you have tests coming up. You will want to make sure to mark upcoming tests on your calendar so that you have enough time to study.

The next important thing to know when preparing for a test is to know what will be on that test. Again, you will need to work with your Guide. You will need to ask what information is the most important to study. Knowing what to study will help you to be prepared for the questions on the test.

What are the two things you need to know when preparing for a test?

1. _____

2. _____

LESSON #87: Preparing for a Test

Estimated Time: 10 minutes

In order to properly prepare for a test, it will take time for you to make sure you learn and know the correct information. Ask your Guide if you have any tests coming up. If you do, make sure to write which days you will have tests on your calendar. Look at how many days you have between today and your next test. Make sure to set aside time on top of your daily lessons to prepare for that test. This might mean that you watch a little less television, or you review your notes instead of playing a video game. These extra few minutes you set aside each day to study and review will add up, and you will feel ready and prepared to tackle the test.

What are some ways you can set aside time to study for a test?

_____
_____
_____
_____
_____

LESSON #88

Preparing for a Test

Estimated Time: 15 minutes

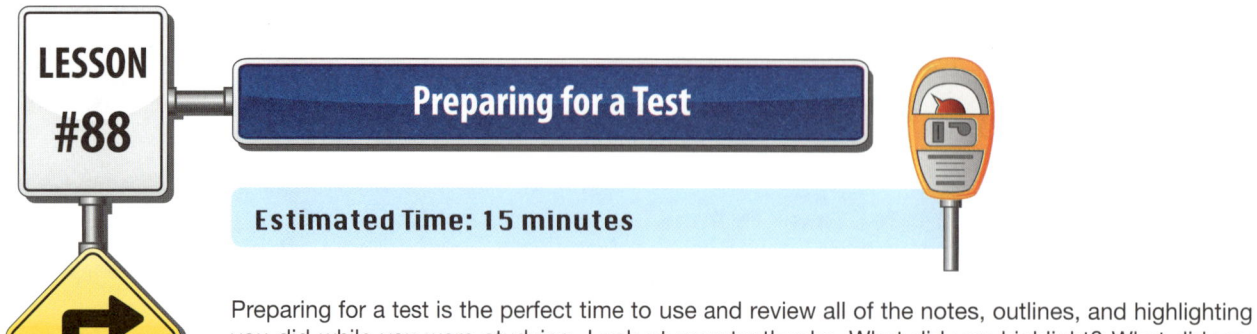

Preparing for a test is the perfect time to use and review all of the notes, outlines, and highlighting you did while you were studying. Look at your textbooks. What did you highlight? What did you write on your sticky notes? You should have written the main ideas. Go back and read these ideas. If there is a concept that you are not clear on, you should go back to your textbook and reread the information about that idea. You could also have a discussion with your Guide about these confusing topics. By reviewing your notes and outlines, you will be able to refresh your memory about what you have learned, which will help you to do better on your next test.

What can you use to prepare for a test?

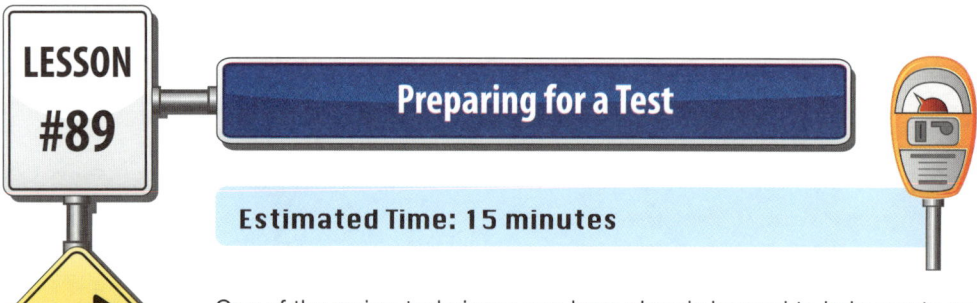

_____
_____
_____
_____
_____

LESSON #89

Preparing for a Test

Estimated Time: 15 minutes

One of the review techniques you have already learned to help you to review for a test is to make up test questions. For your next test, try this strategy to help you think about what might be on the test. First, ask your Guide what areas you should prepare for. Then, working alone or with your Guide, look at your textbook and notes and create your own test questions. Then, take your own test. Check your answers with your Guide. If you missed a question, this is something that you will need to review and practice before taking the test.

Making your own test questions is a great way to prepare for the real thing!

LESSON #90

Preparing for a Test

Estimated Time: 15 minutes

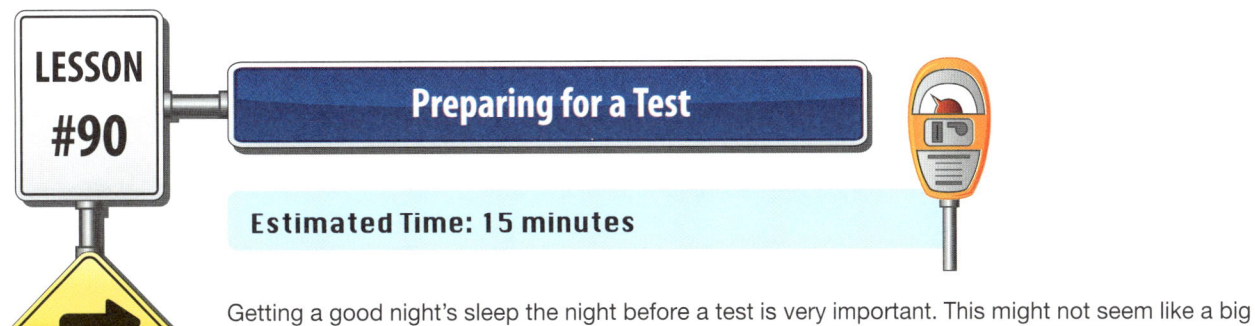

Getting a good night's sleep the night before a test is very important. This might not seem like a big deal, but it really can help you do your best. If you are up too late, you may be tired. If you are tired, you won't be able to focus on your work. When you are rested, you can think clearly, which will help you do better.

The morning of a test, make sure to eat a good breakfast. Fueling your body with healthy food helps your brain to function at its best. Good things to eat for breakfast are fruit, oatmeal, eggs, or toast. Sugary foods like donuts are not the best to eat because the sugar will give you a little bit of energy right away, but you will soon be sluggish. Eating a healthy breakfast will give you energy to make it through the whole test.

Before your next test, try these two strategies to help improve your grades.

LESSON #91: Multiple Choice Questions

Estimated Time: 15 minutes

There are many different ways that a test question can be asked. For the next couple weeks, you will learn about different kinds of test questions, tips to help you answer those questions, and then practice answering questions in all four subjects. This week, you will learn about the most common type of test question—the multiple choice question.

A multiple choice question asks one question and gives three or four choices for an answer. To answer the question, you will choose the best answer. Many times, you will be able to tell right away that one answer is wrong. Let's take a look at an example of a multiple choice question and how you can come to the answer.

$$32 + 17 =$$

A. 4
B. 59
C. 49
D. 94

The first thing to do is to look at the question. Since this example is a math question, estimate an answer in your head. Right away, you should be able to eliminate, or get rid of, at least two answers. You know that 4 cannot be an answer because this is an addition problem, and the number answer needs to be larger than the numbers that are being added. Cross out answer *A* with your pencil. You should also be able to tell that answer *D* is not correct. 94 is too high. Use your pencil to cross that answer out. That leaves you with the answers 59 and 49. One of those must be correct. Now, you should solve the problem. You may need a piece of scratch paper or graph paper to solve the problem. When you solve it, you will see that 49 is the correct answer. On a standardized test, you will need to color in the circle of the correct answer, so color in the circle with the letter *C* as that is the correct answer. Crossing out answers to narrow your choices down to two is called the process of elimination.

This week, you will continue to practice answering multiple choice questions in each of the different subjects.

LESSON #92

Language Arts Multiple Choice Questions

Estimated Time: 15 minutes

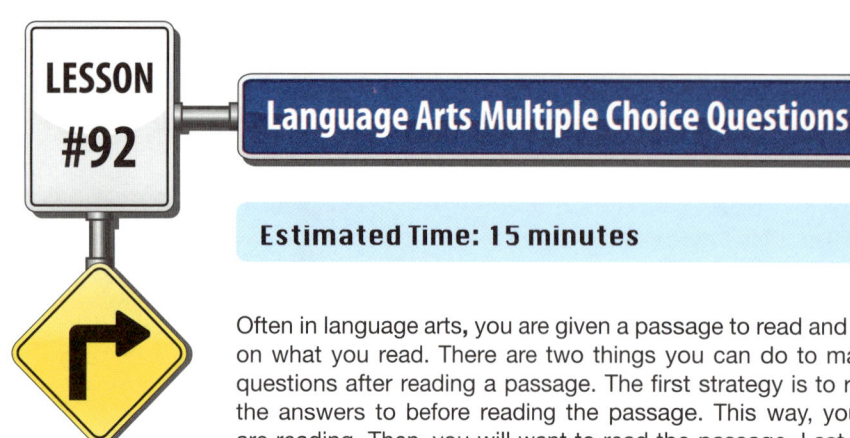

Often in language arts, you are given a passage to read and then you must answer questions based on what you read. There are two things you can do to make it easier to answer multiple choice questions after reading a passage. The first strategy is to read the questions you will have to find the answers to before reading the passage. This way, you know what to think about while you are reading. Then, you will want to read the passage. Last, you will start to answer the questions. Carefully, read each question. If you are not sure of the answer, go back and reread the passage to look for the answer. Make sure to cross out the answers you know are incorrect.

Let's practice.

Read the following paragraph and answer the questions:

> Soaring above the sandy beach he could see cans, paper, bottles, and many other forms of litter lying around. He was amazed to see the beach that way. It looked much dirtier than just looking around his little space on the shore. He could even see some trash floating in the water as it washed back out to sea.

Which of the following is an accurate description of the beach?

A. It was sandy, clean, and bright.
B. It was dirty with trash everywhere.
C. It had seashells and kids playing in the water.

Read the question again. What does the question want to know? It wants to know what the beach looked like. If you need to, go back and reread the paragraph to look for the information you need. Once you have found the information in the passage, underline it. Then, look at the answer choices. Cross out the ones that you know are wrong. Circle the answer that is correct.

The correct answer is *B*. Did you get the correct answer? Turn to page 171 of Section Two. Read the passage and answer questions 1 – 4.

LESSON #93

Math Multiple Choice Questions

Estimated Time: 15 minutes

On a math test, you can also answer multiple choice questions. To solve these questions, you should first look to see which operation you will need to use, like addition or subtraction. Then, do the problem on a piece of scratch paper. Look for the correct answer. If you don't see your answer, go back and do the problem again. Be very careful! Sometimes, an answer choice will be listed that could be correct if you had made a mistake, such as adding when you are supposed to subtract. You will want to double check your answer before choosing the correct one.

Try an example.

Subtract. Circle your answer.

1. $98 - 32 =$

    A. 56
    B. 130
    C. 57
    D. 66

Which answer did you choose? If you chose *D*, you are correct!

LESSON #94

Math Multiple Choice Questions

Estimated Time: 15 minutes

Sometimes on a test, you might see *all of the above* as an answer choice. This means that all of the answer choices given are correct. As you read the question and then look at your answer choices, if you realize that two or more choices could be the answer, then choosing *all of the above* is a good idea. But, be careful, sometimes that answer choice is given just to trick you.

Let's take a look at an example.

1. Which of the following are examples of a solid?

    A. book
    B. apple
    C. guitar
    D. all of the above

Read the question. Ask yourself: *What is a solid?* A solid is something with a definite shape. Look at the answer choices: book, apple, guitar, and all of the above. All of these are solids, so you know that *all of the above* is the correct choice. You should circle *D* as the correct answer.

Turn to page 175 in Section Two. Complete questions 1 – 4.

LESSON #95

Social Studies Multiple Choice Questions

Estimated Time: 15 minutes

Test questions are written to make you think. Sometimes the answer will come to you right away. Other times, you may have to read the question a few times, and you will have to stop and think. Remember the strategies you have learned this week. Carefully read the question and cross off the answers you know are wrong. Then, look at the answers you have left and make your best choice.

Use these skills to answer the question below.

1. Which of the following is NOT a continent?

    A. Australia
    B. Europe
    C. Canada
    D. Africa

The correct answer is *C*. Did you see in the question you were supposed to find which one did not fit into the group? The question asks about continents, so you have to remind yourself what a continent is. Look at your choices. Canada is the name of country, which is not the same as a continent. This must the correct answer because Canada is not a continent.

Turn to page 187 in Section Two. Answer questions 1 – 4.

Lesson #96: Answering Comprehension Questions

Estimated Time: 15 minutes

One type of question that you will commonly be asked, especially in reading, is the comprehension question. Comprehension questions are designed to see how much you understood in the passage you read. This week, you will learn and practice some tips to help make it easier for you to answer comprehension questions.

When you are given a reading passage and questions to answer, you might think that you should just read the passage first. The first thing you should actually do is read the questions you will have to answer. By reading the questions first, you are setting your purpose for reading. You are getting ready to think about the information you are looking for while reading.

This week, you will work with the same reading passage and questions, then you will learn step-by-step how to answer these questions. Below are the questions you will need to answer. Read them. The reading passage is not given today because your first step is to read the questions.

1. What month does this story take place?
    A. August
    B. September
    C. October
    D. November

2. What is Mrs. Okocho's favorite hobby?
    A. playing cards
    B. shopping
    C. babysitting Latasha
    D. gardening

3. Select the place Ella was standing when Latasha said, "Get away from there!"
    A. in Mrs. Okocho's flowerbed
    B. in a muddy puddle
    C. on the staircase
    D. on the sidewalk

What is the name of the school Latasha goes to? What grade is she in? Answer in a complete sentence. _____
_____
_____

Tomorrow, you will read a short passage, and begin to answer these questions.

LESSON #97

Answering Comprehension Questions

Estimated Time: 15 minutes

The first step in answering a comprehension question is to see whether it is a multiple choice question or not. Yesterday you read the questions you will need to answer. The second step is to then read the passage. Today, you will read an excerpt from *Latasha and the Little Red Tornado*. While you read, think about the questions you will need to answer.

"Ella Fitzgerald Gandy!" I cried. It was the day after Labor Day, a sunny September Tuesday, and we were standing on the sidewalk in front of the house.

I had just gotten home from the after-school program at Cedarville Elementary. I just started third grade there last week. I was about to take Ella for a walk down the block. But Ella had another idea. She wanted to eat some of Mrs. Okocho's daisies.

Mrs. Okocho is our downstairs neighbor. She comes from a country called Nigeria. That's in Africa. She is quite elderly—which is a nice way of saying *old*. Momma says it's rude to call people old.

Ella was standing with three paws in the flowerbed and one on the pavement. "Get away from there!" I hissed, glancing nervously in the first floor window.

In most ways, Mrs. Okocho does not act old, or elderly, or even like a grown-up. She has a loud, high-pitched laugh that sounds like a kid being tickled, and a silly sense of humor to match. But there is one thing, and one thing only, that she is deadly serious about: her flowers. She grows them in a big flowerbed in front of the porch. Her favorites are her daisies. They are light purple with tight petals that make me think of an opened-up muffin wrapper.

Maybe that was why Ella had chosen to lick them as if they had a treat hidden in the stem.

LESSON #98

Answering Comprehension Questions

Estimated Time: 15 minutes

Now that you have read the questions and the passage, you can begin to answer the questions. Read each question again. If you know that an answer is definitely wrong, cross it out. This should leave you with two or three answers left for you to think about. Today, look at questions 1, 2, and 3, and cross out the answers you know are definitely not correct. You will answer the questions tomorrow.

"Ella Fitzgerald Gandy!" I cried. It was the day after Labor Day, a sunny September Tuesday, and we were standing on the sidewalk in front of the house.

I had just gotten home from the after-school program at Cedarville Elementary. I just started third grade there last week. I was about to take Ella for a walk down the block. But Ella had another idea. She wanted to eat some of Mrs. Okocho's daisies.

Mrs. Okocho is our downstairs neighbor. She comes from a country called Nigeria. That's in Africa. She is quite elderly—which is a nice way of saying *old*. Momma says it's rude to call people old.

DETOUR NEXT PAGE

END DETOUR

Ella was standing with three paws in the flowerbed and one on the pavement. "Get away from there!" I hissed, glancing nervously in the first floor window.

In most ways, Mrs. Okocho does not act old, or elderly, or even like a grown-up. She has a loud, high-pitched laugh that sounds like a kid being tickled, and a silly sense of humor to match. But there is one thing, and one thing only, that she is deadly serious about: her flowers. She grows them in a big flowerbed in front of the porch. Her favorites are her daisies. They are light purple with tight petals that make me think of an opened-up muffin wrapper.

Maybe that was why Ella had chosen to lick them as if they had a treat hidden in the stem.

1. What month does this story take place?
   A. August
   B. September
   C. October
   D. November

2. What is Mrs. Okocho's favorite hobby?
   A. playing cards
   B. shopping
   C. babysitting Latasha
   D. gardening

3. Select the place Ella was standing when Latasha said, "Get away from there!"
   A. in Mrs. Okocho's flowerbed
   B. in a muddy puddle
   C. on the staircase
   D. on the sidewalk

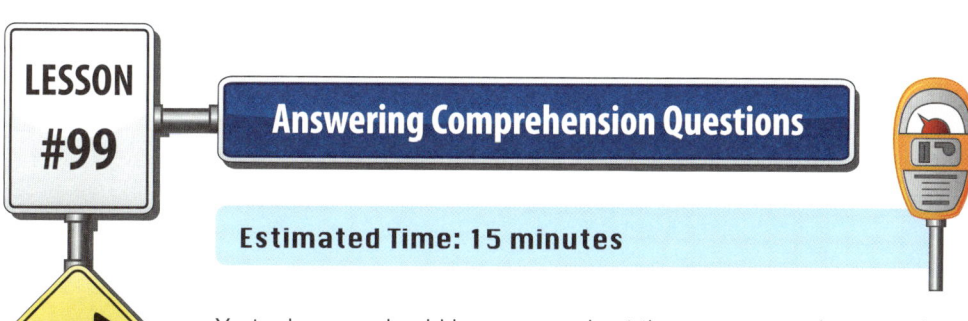

LESSON #99

Answering Comprehension Questions

Estimated Time: 15 minutes

Yesterday, you should have crossed out the answers you know are incorrect. Today, you will need to use the reading passage to help you answer the questions. Read each question and then go back and find the answer in the reading. For example, look at question 1. You are supposed to find out which month this story takes place. Go back to the beginning of the passage, and look for the answer. Once you find the answer, underline it with your pencil, or highlight it with a highlighter. You would underline or highlight September in the second sentence. This is your answer. Now, you can answer this question by circling the correct answer.

Answer the remaining questions about the passage. Make sure to highlight or underline the answer in the reading passage. For question 4, you will have to write an answer. Make sure to answer the question in a complete sentence.

DETOUR NEXT PAGE

END DETOUR

"Ella Fitzgerald Gandy!" I cried. It was the day after Labor Day, a sunny September Tuesday, and we were standing on the sidewalk in front of the house.

I had just gotten home from the after-school program at Cedarville Elementary. I just started third grade there last week. I was about to take Ella for a walk down the block. But Ella had another idea. She wanted to eat some of Mrs. Okocho's daisies.

Mrs. Okocho is our downstairs neighbor. She comes from a country called Nigeria. That's in Africa. She is quite elderly—which is a nice way of saying *old*. Momma says it's rude to call people old.

Ella was standing with three paws in the flowerbed and one on the pavement. "Get away from there!" I hissed, glancing nervously in the first floor window.

In most ways, Mrs. Okocho does not act old, or elderly, or even like a grown-up. She has a loud, high-pitched laugh that sounds like a kid being tickled, and a silly sense of humor to match. But there is one thing, and one thing only, that she is deadly serious about: her flowers. She grows them in a big flowerbed in front of the porch. Her favorites are her daisies. They are light purple with tight petals that make me think of an opened-up muffin wrapper.

Maybe that was why Ella had chosen to lick them as if they had a treat hidden in the stem.

1. What month does this story take place?
   A. August
   B. September
   C. October
   D. November

2. What is Mrs. Okocho's favorite hobby?
   A. playing cards
   B. shopping
   C. babysitting Latasha
   D. gardening

3. Select the place Ella was standing when Latasha said, "Get away from there!"
   A. in Mrs. Okocho's flowerbed
   B. in a muddy puddle
   C. on the staircase
   D. on the sidewalk

What is the name of the school Latasha goes to? What grade is she in? Answer in a complete sentence. _____

_____

_____

LESSON #100

Answering Comprehension Questions

Estimated Time: 15 minutes

Throughout this week, you have learned some strategies to help you answer comprehension questions. Today, you will put everything together to answer a few questions on your own.

Think about the steps and strategies to answer the questions below. Read the passage and then circle the correct answer.

> On Saturday, Jay and Garrett arrived fifteen minutes early. The race was in the Sierra foothills. They would be on mostly flat land, but the little rolling hills would be all around, with the great low mountains of the Sierra Nevada rising in the east. The smell of dry, July earth was overpowering; it was almost like being in a barn full of hay.
>
> Rubin was waiting for them, beside a buckeye tree in which a vulture sat on one of the low branches.
>
> "Good luck, Jay. I know you'll be fine," Garrett said. "Look, I hope you don't mind, but I invited a few others, okay? I didn't want to stand here and wait by myself," he said, smiling, "and I thought you could use the support."
>
> Jay looked around and saw their friends Fiona and Arnie walking toward them. They said hello and wished him luck.
>
> "I guess he doesn't have anyone to come and watch," Garrett said quietly, looking toward Rubin.
>
> "Yeah, I guess not. I should probably go," Jay said. He walked toward Rubin and felt his stomach begin to twist and his heart begin to knock at his chest. He tried to control his breathing.

1. Where does the race take place?
    A. in the eastern Sierra Nevada mountains
    B. at Jay's house
    C. on the foothills of the Sierras
    D. in a barn

2. Who came to watch Jay compete in the race?
    A. Garret
    B. Rubin
    C. Fiona and Arnie
    D. all of the above

3. How does Jay feel before the race begins?
    A. excited
    B. tired
    C. doesn't care
    D. nervous

What season is this race taking place? How do you know? Answer in complete sentences.

_____
_____
_____

WEEK 21

LESSON #101: Context Clues

Estimated Time: 15 minutes

Context clues are an important skill to know how to use. You can use context clues to help you figure out the meaning of a word you don't know. When you use context clues, you are using the words around the unknown word to help you figure out the meaning.

Let's look at an example of how using context clues can help you figure out the meaning of a word.

In the distance, Patrick saw a beautiful and graceful bird <u>soaring</u> high in the sky.

What does the word *soaring* mean? Look at the words around it. Try to use them to help you figure out what the words mean. You know the sentence is talking about a bird. How do birds move in the sky? They fly. So, *soaring* must mean that the bird is flying in the sky.

Throughout this week, you will see how you can use context clues in every subject, even math.

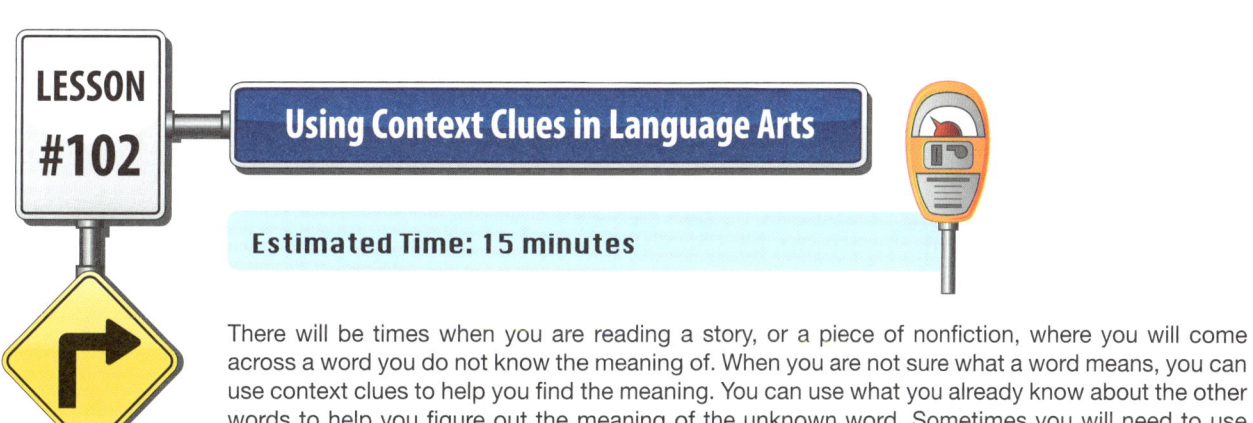

LESSON #102: Using Context Clues in Language Arts

Estimated Time: 15 minutes

There will be times when you are reading a story, or a piece of nonfiction, where you will come across a word you do not know the meaning of. When you are not sure what a word means, you can use context clues to help you find the meaning. You can use what you already know about the other words to help you figure out the meaning of the unknown word. Sometimes you will need to use clues from some of the other sentences near this unknown word. Look at this example from "Cell Phones: Past, Present, and Future."

They have become very important to people's lives. Many do not consider their cell phone a luxury, but a <u>necessity</u>.

Using the other words and sentences above, can you figure out what the word *necessity* means? Some clues might be *very important,* and you know the meaning is opposite of *luxury*. Using these two pieces of information, you should be able to determine that *necessity* means something you need or have to have.

Turn to page 172 in Section Two. Complete questions 5 – 8 to practice using context clues.

LESSON #103: Using Context Clues in Math

Estimated Time: 15 minutes

You might think that it would be difficult to use context clues in math, but in word problems there are special words that tell you which operation you will need to use. These can be called context clues, or even keywords. These words may be something like *how many in all*, *how many more than*, *in total*, or *less*.

Here is an example of using context clues in a math word problem.

Jillian has 12 gummy fish. Her sister, Courtney, has 14 gummy fish. How many in all do the two girls have?

Did you see the keywords that tell you what you need to do? Go back to the problem and underline the words *in all*. *In all* means to add. Go ahead and add 12 + 14 to find how many gummy fish the sisters have.

12 + 14 = 26 gummy fish
Did you get the correct answer?

Turn to page 175 of Section Two. Look for the keywords in problems 5 – 8, and then solve each problem.

LESSON #104: Using Context Clues in Science

Estimated Time: 15 minutes

There are many new vocabulary words for you to learn in science because it is a subject that has a lot of specific words and meanings. Many times you can get a good idea of what a word means based on what other words it looks like. Take the word *igneous*, for example. This word begins like the word *ignite*, which means to light on fire. You can use what you know about this word to help you remember that an igneous rock is a rock that is made of lava (which is hotter than fire) that has cooled. In science, you will want to look at words that are unfamiliar to you to see if it looks like a familiar word to help you get the meaning.

Turn to page 181 of Section Two. Complete questions 5 – 8.

LESSON #105

Using Context Clues in Social Studies

Estimated Time: 15 minutes

Using context clues in social studies is the same as in language arts. You will use the words surrounding the unknown word to try to figure out a meaning.

Look at the example below.

Sometimes there are civil conflicts, which are problems that happen within the country.

What does the word *civil* mean in this sentence? Look at the other words in the sentence. *Civil* means things that take place within our country. You were able to use what the sentence told you to figure out what another word means.

Practice using context clues to tell the meaning of words on page 187 in Section Two. Complete numbers 5 – 8.

LESSON #106: Reading Essay Questions

Estimated Time: 5 minutes

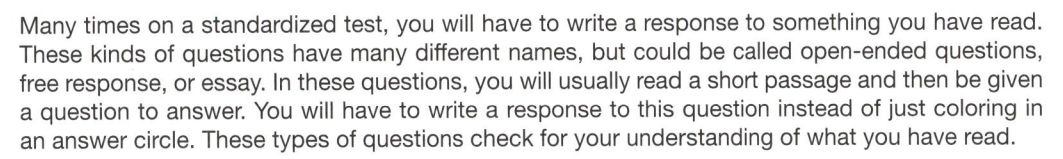

Many times on a standardized test, you will have to write a response to something you have read. These kinds of questions have many different names, but could be called open-ended questions, free response, or essay. In these questions, you will usually read a short passage and then be given a question to answer. You will have to write a response to this question instead of just coloring in an answer circle. These types of questions check for your understanding of what you have read.

Throughout this week, you will learn the steps you will need to take in order to properly answer one of these questions.

LESSON #107: Answering a Reading Essay Question

Estimated Time: 15 minutes

Today, you will begin to write a response to an open-ended reading question. Just like when you answer a comprehension question, the first step is to read the question. This way you can think about answering this question while reading the passage.

Below, you will find a reading passage and a question. Read the question first, and then read the story.

It's a Dog's Life
by Debbie Parrish

Just after Little Dog's birthday he and his family moved to a new part of town. Little Dog had gotten a new laptop computer for his birthday. He was so thrilled you could hear his howls of joy for miles. He immediately went to his room to set up his page on LapBook, a social networking site.

First off, he made his brother one of his LapBook friends, and then he added both of his parents. It was such fun for Little Dog that he began adding all of the dogs from his old neighborhood. The more "friends" he added to his LapBook site, the more excited he got!

Mother and Father Dog said to Little Dog, "Why don't you go outside and play? You need to meet some new dogs."

Little Dog replied, "I will later. Right now I am talking to my friends online."

One day, a big dog from down the street stopped by. "I thought you might like to go for a walk," Big Dog told Little Dog.

But Little Dog said, "I will another day, thank you. Today I am busy on my computer."

"You really need to get out and run around the neighborhood, Little Dog," said his older brother. "You are getting very out of shape staying on that computer all the time. Everyone needs to get exercise to stay healthy. Besides, how are you ever going to meet any new friends here?"

DETOUR NEXT PAGE

END DETOUR

"I will," promised Little Dog. "I just need to get a few more LapBook friends signed up first."

Another morning the dog next door came by Little Dog's house and said, "Would you like to go with me to see my friend, Hound Dog? He broke his paw and is having to stay off of it for a while. I'm going to go over and try to cheer him up. I thought we might play some board games with him."

Little Dog said, "No thanks, I'm going to just hang around here and find out what's happening on LapBook. I have so many friends who I need to find out about.

Day after day, Little Dog was reminded and invited to get out of the house, get some exercise, and meet new friends. But every day he just continued to find more excuses to stay on his computer. He now had over one hundred LapBook friends.

Then, one day, Little Dog felt a tingling in his legs. "Oh no," he yelped. "My legs have gone to sleep!" He decided that maybe it was a good idea to get out of the house and walk some.

He went to the park and saw a group of dogs he had added as friends on his LapBook page. "Hi," said Little Dog to one of them. "What's up?"

The other dog said, "We were just leaving to go to a birthday party for one of our friends. Bye!" And the small group of dogs trotted away.

Little Dog thought to himself, "That would have been fun. I wonder why I wasn't invited."

Then Little Dog spotted a couple of dogs across the park. Again, he recognized them as pictures on his LapBook list. He trotted over and found them playing chase.

"May I play, too?" asked Little Dog.

"We don't know you!" they said. "We're not allowed to play with strangers."

Little Dog looked puzzled. "But you are my friend on LapBook," he whined.

"That's different," one dog said.

"We don't *really* know you," said another.

Quickly the dogs ran away, leaving Little Dog all alone. Little Dog decided to just go home. He walked down the street toward his house. When he passed the big yellow house on the corner, there was a young dog outside with his paw wrapped in a bandage. He was limping as he walked.

"What happened to you?" Little Dog asked.

The dog replied, "I broke my paw. The vet is finally letting me outside to walk on it. I was so bored stuck inside."

Then Little Dog realized that this dog must be Hound Dog. He remembered the day he was asked to go and visit him. Little Dog felt ashamed that he had not come. He started to think about how many dogs he really knew in his new neighborhood and could not come up with even one name.

Hound Dog said, "I'd better go inside now. Mom told me not to stay out very long. Would you like to come in and have some treats with me?"

Little Dog did not hesitate. "Yes, I sure would! Then, maybe, we could play some board games!"

Today, Little Dog had learned a valuable lesson: **To have a friend, you have to be one!**

Give a summary of "It's a Dog's Life" in your own words. Make sure to give examples from the beginning, middle, and end of the story.

LESSON #108

Answering a Reading Essay Question

Estimated Time: 15 minutes

Yesterday, you read an example of an open-ended question. You also read the story that you are supposed to respond to. Before you write your response, you will want to take a pencil or a highlighter and underline or highlight exactly what you are supposed to do.

Look at the question below. What are you asked to do? You will have to give a summary. As you remember, a summary gives the main details of the story. Notice that the question asks you to give examples from the beginning, middle, and end. You will need at least three sentences in your response.

You will want to underline or highlight *summary* and *give examples from the beginning, middle, and end* in the question. This will help remind you what you will need to do in order to properly answer this question.

Give a summary of "It's a Dog's Life" in your own words. Make sure to give examples from the beginning, middle, and end of the story.

_____
_____
_____
_____
_____
_____
_____
_____
_____

LESSON #109

Answering a Reading Essay Question

Estimated Time: 15 minutes

The next step in answering an open-ended reading question is to plan out what you want to write. You have already underlined what you are supposed to do to answer the question. Start writing your ideas on a piece of scratch paper so you know what you want to include in the answer. If you need to, go back to the reading passage to get details. On your scratch paper, you should jot down a few ideas about the main idea of the passage. You will also want to find a detail from the beginning, middle, and end of the story. Planning your essay on a separate sheet of paper allows you to think about what you want to say before you write your final answer.

Take a few moments to plan out your answer ideas. Tomorrow, you will write your final response.

LESSON #110

Answering a Reading Essay Question

Estimated Time: 15 minutes

Yesterday, you planned out the main ideas of your response. Today, you will write your final answer in the response box. Notice how the response box has a line around the question. Anything you want to be read and graded must be written within that box. Anything written outside of the response box will not be graded.

Write your response to the question in the response box below. When you are finished, double check your answer to make sure it answers all of the things you were asked. If needed, go back to the story to help you write your answer.

Give a summary of "It's a Dog's Life" in your own words. Make sure to give examples from the beginning, middle, and end of the story.
_____
_____
_____
_____
_____
_____
_____
_____

Solving Math Word Problems

Estimated Time: 15 minutes

At this point in the school year, you have probably learned about words problems and how to solve them. This week will serve as a review for you. Many times on standardized tests, you will need to solve word problems. Word problems are based on real-life situations, things you might come across in your own life.

A good word problem must have all of the right elements so that you can solve it. The problem must give you enough information, and it must ask you a question. Word problems use special keywords or clues to tell you whether you should add or subtract.

The following words tell you to add:
- add
- altogether
- both
- in all
- sum
- total

The following words tell you to subtract:
- difference
- fewer
- how many more than
- left
- less
- minus
- remains
- subtract

Read each word problem carefully so you know which operation to use.

Read the three problems below. Underline the keywords. On the line, write whether you will need to add or subtract. You do not need to solve the problem.

1. In the first quarter, the Wildcats scored 7 points. In the second quarter, they scored 14 points. How many points did the Wildcats score by halftime? _____

2. Conner and Cooper went to Fun Zone on Saturday. Conner earned 23 tokens. Cooper scored 42 tokens. How many more tokens did Cooper earn than Conner? _____

3. Kelsie's mom bought 1 dozen bananas. In one week, Kelsie and her sister ate 8 bananas. How many are left? (hint: 1 dozen = 12) _____

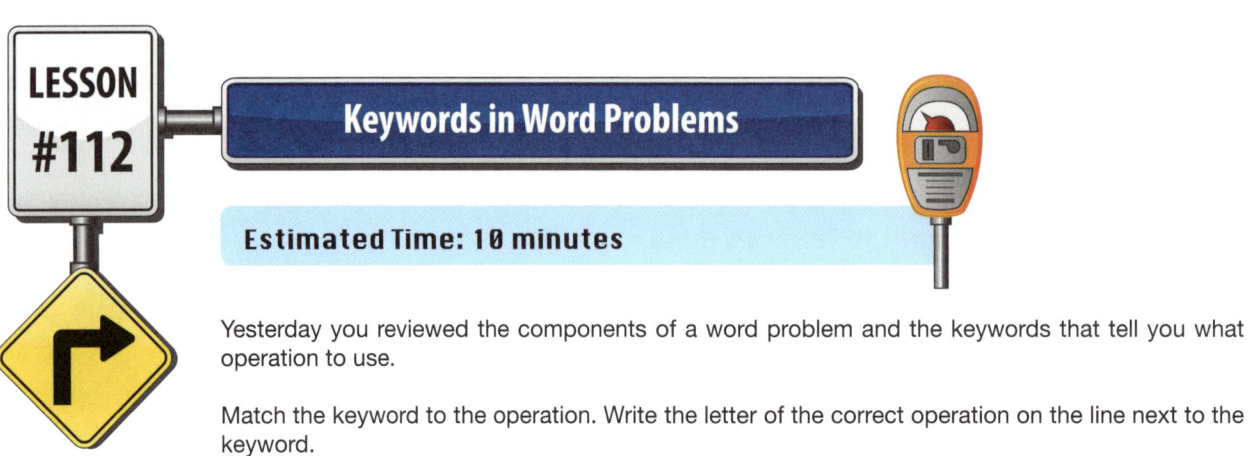

LESSON #112: Keywords in Word Problems

Estimated Time: 10 minutes

Yesterday you reviewed the components of a word problem and the keywords that tell you what operation to use.

Match the keyword to the operation. Write the letter of the correct operation on the line next to the keyword.

____ 1. how many more than   A. addition

____ 2. less   B. addition

____ 3. in all   C. subtraction

____ 4. remaining   D. subtraction

____ 5. total   E. addition

____ 6. sum of   F. subtraction

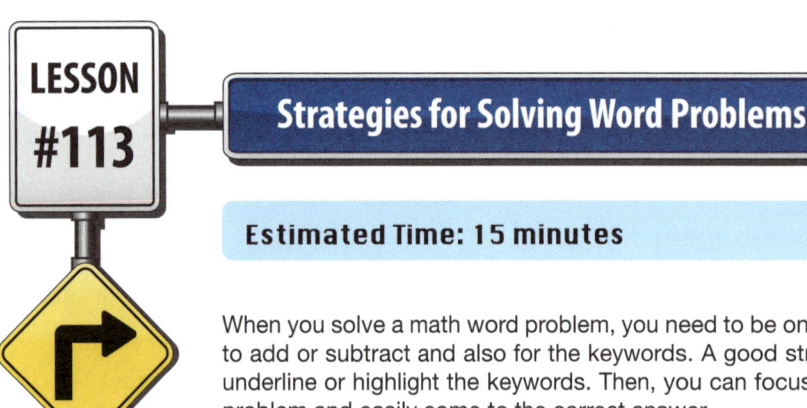

LESSON #113: Strategies for Solving Word Problems

Estimated Time: 15 minutes

When you solve a math word problem, you need to be on the lookout for the numbers you will need to add or subtract and also for the keywords. A good strategy to use is to circle the numbers and underline or highlight the keywords. Then, you can focus on the important information in the word problem and easily come to the correct answer.

Let's take a look at an example.

> The Titanville Tigers scored 43 points in Sunday's game. The Marysburg Marauders scored 68 points. How many more points did the Marauders score than the Tigers?

The two numbers you will need to solve this problem are 43 and 68. Circle them. The keywords are *how many more points*. This means you will need to subtract. Underline or highlight it. Now you can focus on using just this information to find the solution.

DETOUR NEXT PAGE

END DETOUR Use the work space below to set up this problem so you can solve it. Find the solution.

Make sure to add a label to your answer. If you are unsure of what to use for a label, ask yourself: *How many what?* The answer to this question is your label.

In a word problem, what should you underline? _____
_____
_____

What should you circle? _____
_____

Why? _____
_____
_____

LESSON #114

Solving Word Problems

Estimated Time: 15 minutes

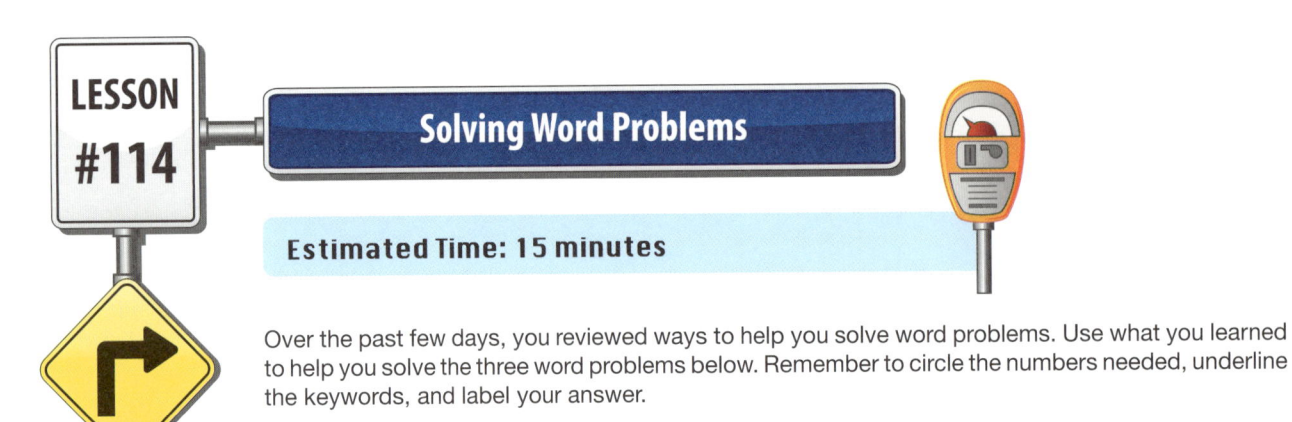

Over the past few days, you reviewed ways to help you solve word problems. Use what you learned to help you solve the three word problems below. Remember to circle the numbers needed, underline the keywords, and label your answer.

1. The orange train traveled 164 miles on its first trip. The blue train traveled 262 miles on its first trip. How many miles total did the two trains travel in all?

2. Sharif collects comic books. Right now, he has 183 comic books. He has decided to give some away to his friends. He gave away 71 comic books. How many does Sharif have left?

3. For breakfast, Marina ate 315 calories. For lunch, she ate 354 calories. By dinnertime, how many calories total has she eaten?

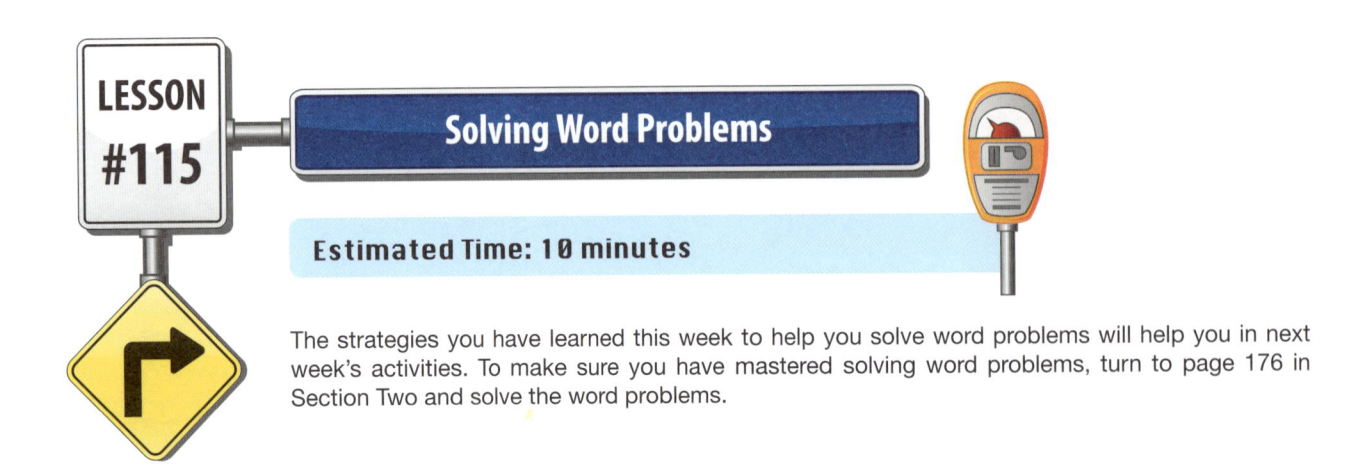

LESSON #115

Solving Word Problems

Estimated Time: 10 minutes

The strategies you have learned this week to help you solve word problems will help you in next week's activities. To make sure you have mastered solving word problems, turn to page 176 in Section Two and solve the word problems.

LESSON #116

Open-Ended Math Problems

Estimated Time: 15 minutes

Two weeks ago, you learned about writing an open-ended response to an essay question in reading. You might not think that you need to write in math, but you do! In math, it is important to be able to explain the steps you took to solve a problem. This week, you will learn how to solve an open-ended problem in math.

The problems you will solve will be word problems. You will have to carefully read the problem and directions to make sure you solve it correctly. Sometimes you will need to add or subtract. Other times you will solve problems that have to do with place value, shapes, or other math ideas. You can use the same tips you learned last week to help you solve the problem. Circle the important numbers and underline the keywords. If there are specific directions, you will underline these, too, so you know what you need to do to answer the problem.

Throughout this week, you will work on solving and answering one open-ended math problem. This is the problem you will solve. All you need to do today is carefully read the problem.

Laurelynn went bowling with her family. Laurelynn had the highest score. Her final score was an even number with three digits.

Write a number that could be Laurelynn's score.
Write the number in the answer box.
Give an explanation of why your answer is correct.

_____
_____
_____
_____
_____
_____
_____
_____

ANSWER BOX:

Lesson #117: Open-Ended Math Problems

Estimated Time: 15 minutes

Yesterday, you read the open-ended math problem you will solve this week. You should read it more than one time to be sure you understand what to do.

Today, you will complete the next step in answering an open-ended problem. After you carefully read the problem, look to see if there are any numbers that you need to circle. In this problem, there are no numbers. You have to choose your own number with this problem.

You will need to underline what you need to do so that you are able to answer the problem correctly. Look at the problem. What do you need to do? You need to write a number that has three digits and is even. Underline that in the problem. You also need to write that number in the answer box. Underline that step. Then, you need to explain why your answer is correct. Underline this direction, too. Is there anything else you need to do? Reread the problem. No, there is nothing else you need to do.

Now that you know exactly what you need to do, you can begin to solve the problem. You will complete this step tomorrow.

Laurelynn went bowling with her family. Laurelynn had the highest score. Her final score was an even number with three digits.

Write a number that could be Laurelynn's score.
Write the number in the answer box.
Give an explanation of why your answer is correct.

_____
_____
_____
_____
_____
_____
_____

ANSWER BOX:

LESSON #118

Open-Ended Math Problems

Estimated Time: 15 minutes

Now that you have done some prep work on your math open-ended problem, you are ready to solve the problem. In your problem, you should have underlined the parts that tell you Laurelynn's score was an even number with three digits, that you need to write the answer in the answer box, and that you need to give an explanation of why your answer is correct.

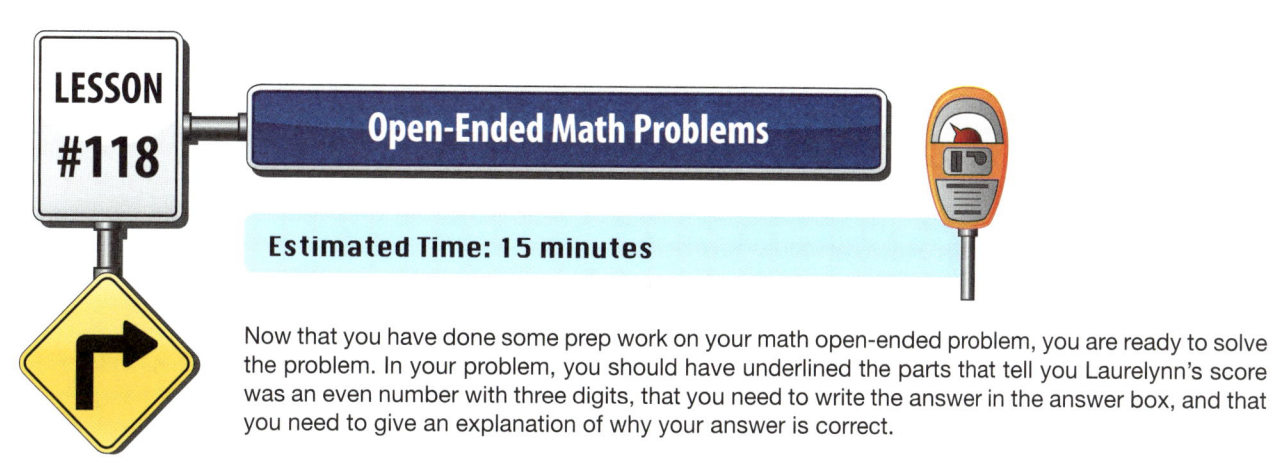

Underline these three things in the problem below so you know what you need to do.

Today, you will complete the first two items. Tomorrow, you will tackle the last step.

Laurelynn went bowling with her family. Laurelynn had the highest score. Her final score was an even number with three digits.

Write a number that could be Laurelynn's score.
Write the number in the answer box.
Give an explanation of why your answer is correct.

_____
_____
_____
_____
_____
_____
_____
_____

ANSWER BOX:

LESSON #119

Open-Ended Math Problems

Estimated Time: 15 minutes

Today, you will complete the open-ended math problem you have been working on. The last step is to explain why your answer is correct. You will need to answer in complete sentences. Your answer should explain why you know the answer you chose is correct.

Today, you will write your explanation on the lines in the answer box. Give as much detail as possible.

Laurelynn went bowling with her family. Laurelynn had the highest score. Her final score was an even number with three digits.

Write a number that could be Laurelynn's score.
Write the number in the answer box.
Give an explanation of why your answer is correct.

_____
_____
_____
_____
_____
_____
_____
_____

ANSWER BOX:

LESSON #120

Open-Ended Math Problems

Estimated Time: 15 minutes

Today, you will use everything you have learned this week about solving an open-ended math problem to solve one on your own. Turn to page 176 of Section Two and complete the problem.

LESSON #121

Time to Take a Test! Now What?

Estimated Time: 15 minutes

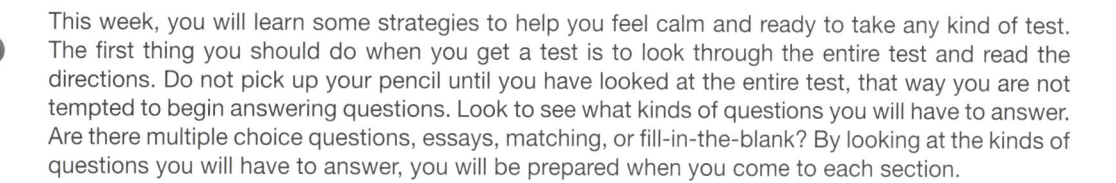

This week, you will learn some strategies to help you feel calm and ready to take any kind of test. The first thing you should do when you get a test is to look through the entire test and read the directions. Do not pick up your pencil until you have looked at the entire test, that way you are not tempted to begin answering questions. Look to see what kinds of questions you will have to answer. Are there multiple choice questions, essays, matching, or fill-in-the-blank? By looking at the kinds of questions you will have to answer, you will be prepared when you come to each section.

What should you do before taking a test? _____
_____
_____

LESSON #122

Time to Take a Test! Now What?

Estimated Time: 15 minutes

After you have looked over the test you are about to take and have read all of the directions, you may find it helpful to take a few minutes to make a checklist of things to do when taking a test. This can help you to stay organized and focused while taking the test so that you do not panic. As you complete each task on your checklist, cross it off. When you come to the end of the test, go back over your checklist to make sure you have completed everything. Here is an example of what a checklist might look like:

- Did I put my name on the test?
- Read directions.
- Answer each section.
- Did I show my work?
- I checked my answers.

A checklist may look different for different types of tests. For example, on a math test, you may want to put *Did I label my answers?* or *Did I use the correct operation?*

The next time you are given a test, try this strategy to help keep you organized and on task!

LESSON #123: Time to Take a Test! Now What?

Estimated Time: 10 minutes

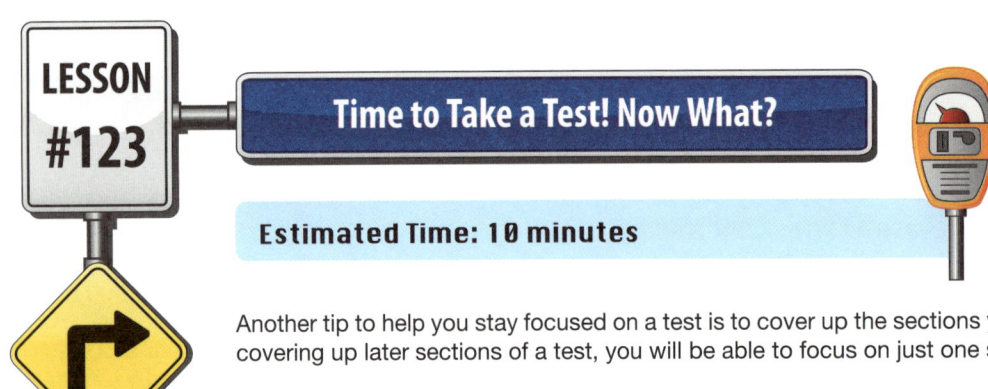

Another tip to help you stay focused on a test is to cover up the sections you have not gotten to. By covering up later sections of a test, you will be able to focus on just one section at a time.

To do this, first look at your test to see how it is set up. Are there many sections, or just a few questions? Then, take a blank sheet of paper and cover up all of the test except for the section that you are working on. As you complete a section, move the blank sheet of paper to reveal the next set of questions.

This is a great strategy to use to help you stay calm and focused when taking a test.

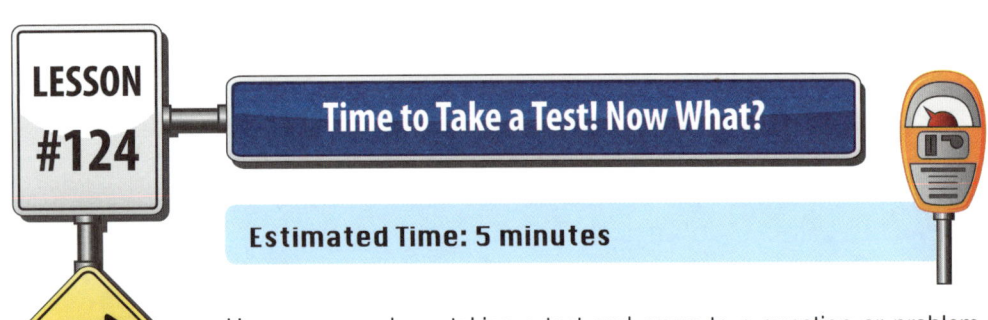

LESSON #124: Time to Take a Test! Now What?

Estimated Time: 5 minutes

Have you ever been taking a test and came to a question or problem you didn't know how to answer? What did you do? Did you panic? Did you get frustrated that you didn't know what to do? If so, then this a great tip for you to use! If you come across a question that you just aren't sure of the answer, then skip it. To help you remember to come back to the question you skipped, you may want to circle the question number, or put a small mark by it. After you have answered all of the questions you know, then go back and focus on the ones you weren't sure of. You will then have plenty of time to spend on the more difficult questions.

The next time you come to a question that you aren't sure of, try out this tip to help you feel more comfortable finding the answer.

LESSON #125: Time to Take a Test! Now What?

Estimated Time: 10 minutes

After you get to the end of a test, go back to the beginning and check to make sure you answered all of the questions and did not skip anything. Then, look over your test questions to make sure you came to the correct answer. If it is a math problem that you found tricky, try it again to make sure you get the same answer. If it is an essay question, reread the question, read your answer, and make sure you fully answered the question.

This will help you to find any small errors or mistakes that you may have made. If you find a mistake, you can fix it before turning it in to be graded.

Why should you check your test before turning it in? _____
_____
_____
_____

LESSON #126

True or False Questions

Estimated Time: 15 minutes

One type of test question that you will often see in all four subjects is the true or false question. A true or false question is a sentence and you have to decide if it is correct (true) or not correct (false). Today, you will learn how to tell if a statement is true or false. Then later in the week, you will practice answering true or false questions in reading, math, science, and social studies.

In order to say that a statement is true, every word in the sentence must be true. For example: *A kitten is a baby cat.* This is a true statement because the entire sentence is true.

If even just one word in a statement is wrong, then the whole sentence is false. For example: *A group of fish is called a pack.* A group of fish is called a school, so the sentence is false.

When you see words like *never*, *always*, and *every* it is usually a clue that the statement is false. For example: *Every child loves fruit.* Not *every* child loves fruit, so this sentence is false.

If you see the words *usually, sometimes,* or *generally* this is a clue that a statement is usually true. However, sometimes these sentences are false. For example: *It usually snows in winter.* This sentence is true. If you live in an area where it is cold, it will snow in the winter time, so this is a correct sentence. These types of questions are tricky because the answer could depend on what you think or feel. These particular true or false questions will take a little more brain power on your part to answer correctly.

Use what you just read to answer the following true or false questions. Write *T* on the line if the sentence is true. Write *F* on the line if the sentence is false.

____ 1. The colors in a rainbow are red, orange, yellow, green, blue, indigo, and violet.

____ 2. All animals need to eat, breathe, and move.

____ 3. Every little girl loves pink.

____ 4. Breakfast is usually eaten in the morning.

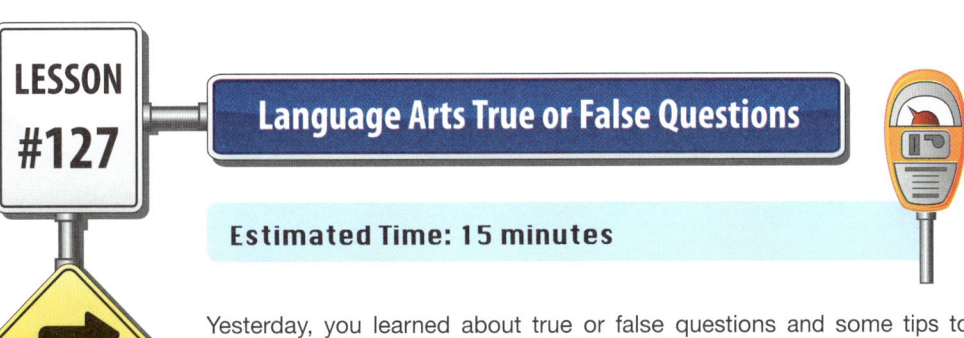

LESSON #127

Language Arts True or False Questions

Estimated Time: 15 minutes

Yesterday, you learned about true or false questions and some tips to help you answer these questions. If you need to, review yesterday's information before turning to page 172 in Section Two to answer true or false questions. When answering the questions, read each statement carefully and think about whether that sentence is correct (true) or incorrect (false).

LESSON #128

Math True or False Questions

Estimated Time: 15 minutes

Answering true or false questions in math is similar to answering them in language arts. You may be asked to tell if the answer to a question is correct, or you may need to think about math vocabulary. To answer these questions, you will need to read each one carefully, think about the problem, and take your time. Let's look at two examples.

$$100 + 20 = 100$$

Is this problem true or false? Take a moment to work the problem out yourself. 100 + 20 = 120, so this problem is not correct. It is false.

Sum is another name for an answer to an addition problem.

Read that statement again. Think about what you know about math vocabulary for addition. What is a sum? It is the answer to an addition problem. Does your answer match with the original statement? Yes, it does. So, this statement is correct, or true.

Turn to page 177 of Section Two and practice the math true or false questions.

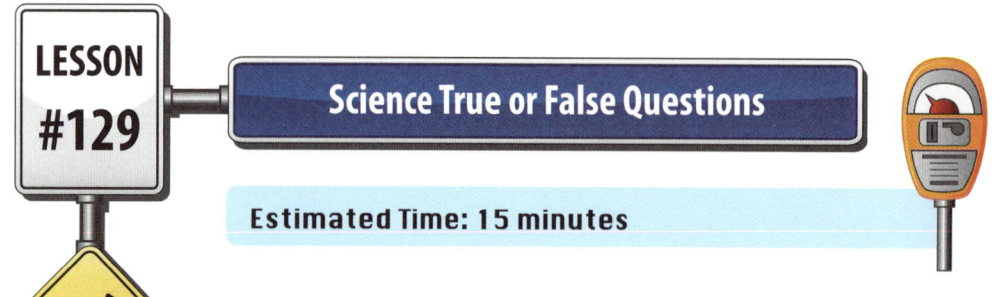

LESSON #129

Science True or False Questions

Estimated Time: 15 minutes

Today, you will practice more true or false questions, but this time they will be focused on science. Like answering any other true or false question, carefully read the question and then think about what you know about the topic. If you see words like *never* or *always,* it may be a clue that the sentence is false. If you see words like *usually* or *sometimes,* then it may be a clue that the sentence is true.

Practice answering true or false questions on page 182 of Section Two.

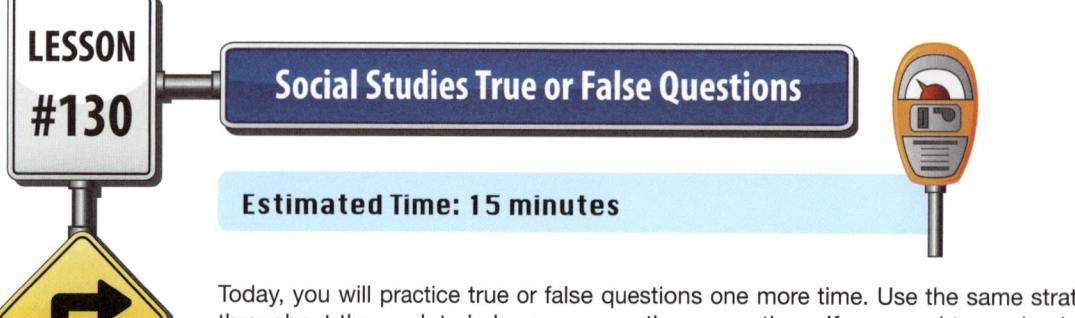

LESSON #130

Social Studies True or False Questions

Estimated Time: 15 minutes

Today, you will practice true or false questions one more time. Use the same strategies you used throughout the week to help you answer these questions. If you need to, go back to the previous lessons to look at the tips for answering true or false questions.

Turn to page 188 in Section Two to practice true or false questions.

WEEK 27

LESSON #131: Matching Questions

Estimated Time: 15 minutes

On a test, matching questions are often used to see if you can match words to definitions, or a word to an idea or concept. Here is an example of what matching questions might look like.

____ 1. sound   A. light hits an object and bounces back

____ 2. reflection   B. the way on which light travels

____ 3. pitch   C. the bending of light

____ 4. refraction   D. something you can hear

____ 5. wavelength   E. how high or low a sound is

This matching quiz is testing you on science vocabulary. When beginning a matching quiz read each of the vocabulary words first. Begin to think about each of the words and what its definition might be. Then read the list of definitions. Answer the questions you know first. For these, you will write the letter of the definition next to the vocabulary word it matches. As you match words and definitions, cross off or mark the definitions with an X so that you know which ones have already been used. You will then be able to narrow down the remaining ones to just a few words. Then think about what you know about each word to figure out the last definitions.

Use these tips to match the vocabulary word to its definition.

Throughout this week, you will practice matching problems in each subject.

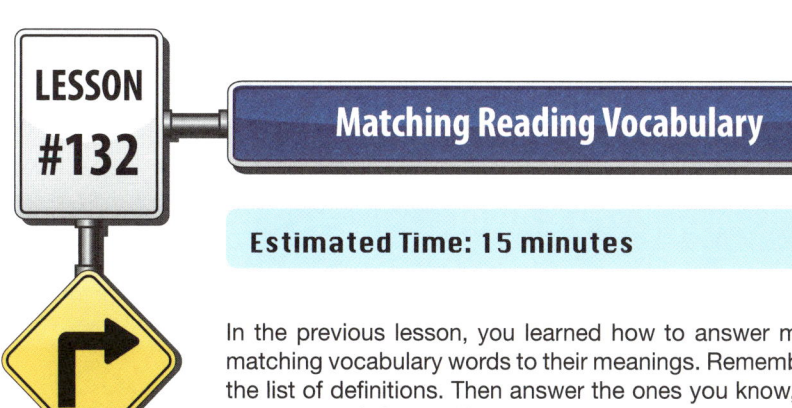

LESSON #132: Matching Reading Vocabulary

Estimated Time: 15 minutes

In the previous lesson, you learned how to answer matching questions. Today, you will practice matching vocabulary words to their meanings. Remember to read each of the words first. Then, read the list of definitions. Then answer the ones you know, and take your time to answer the ones you are unsure of. Cross off, or mark with an X, each definition as you go.

Turn to page 173 in Section Two to answer the matching questions.

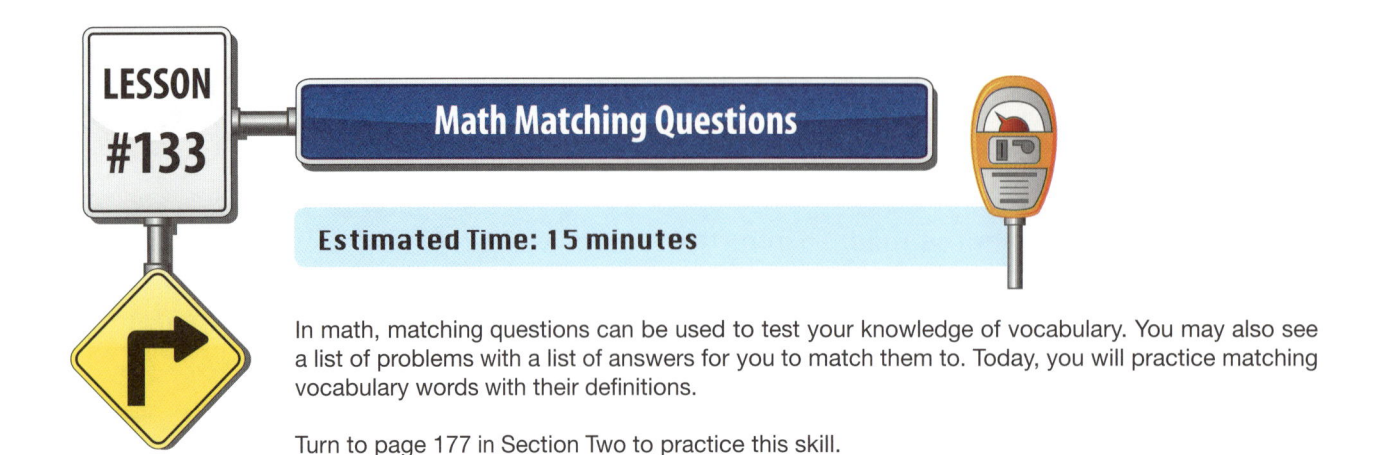

LESSON #133: Math Matching Questions

Estimated Time: 15 minutes

In math, matching questions can be used to test your knowledge of vocabulary. You may also see a list of problems with a list of answers for you to match them to. Today, you will practice matching vocabulary words with their definitions.

Turn to page 177 in Section Two to practice this skill.

LESSON #134: Science Matching Questions

Estimated Time: 15 minutes

So far this week, you have practiced matching reading and math vocabulary words. Hopefully, you have found a method that works best for you when solving this type of question.

Turn to page 182 in Section Two to practice matching vocabulary.

LESSON #135: Social Studies Matching Questions

Estimated Time: 15 minutes

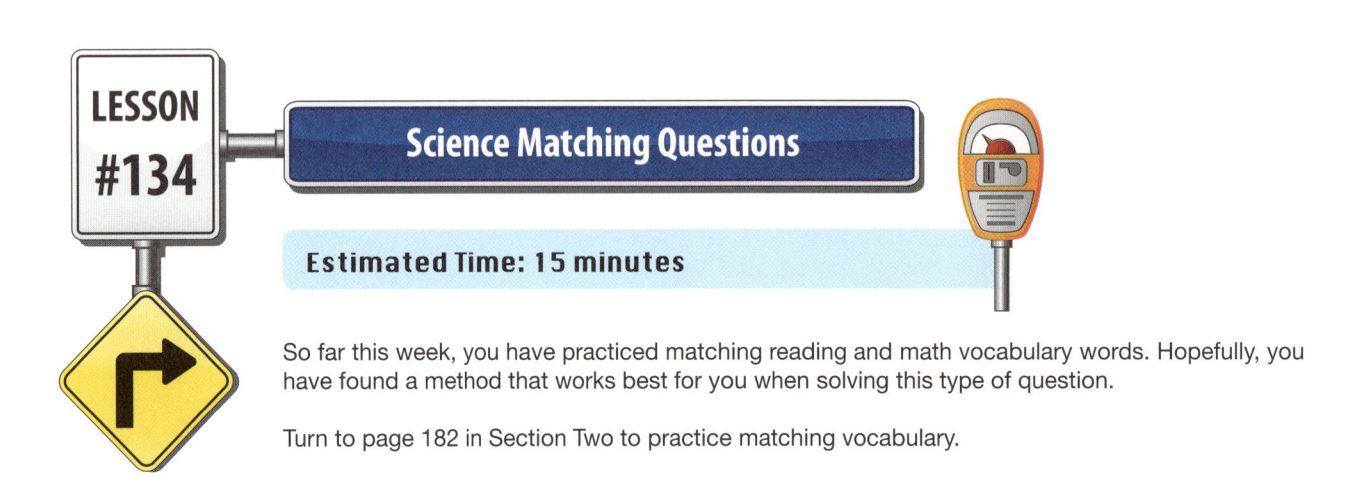

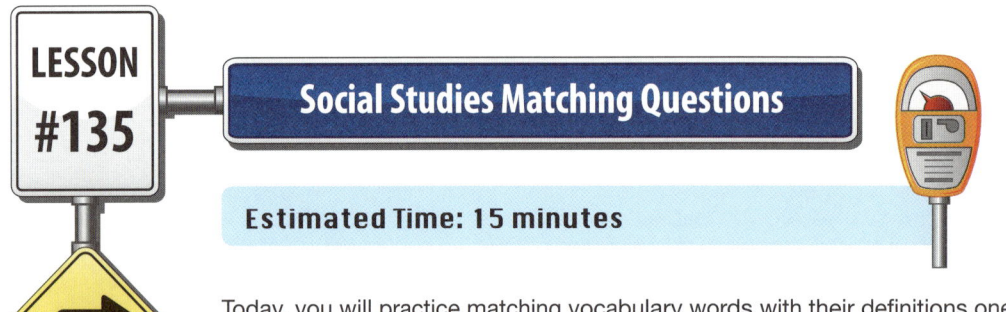

Today, you will practice matching vocabulary words with their definitions one last time. Continue to use the same strategy you have used throughout the week. Read the words first, and then read the definitions. Match the words to the definitions that you automatically know. As you match the words and definitions, cross out the definitions that you have already used.

Turn to page 188 of Section Two to practice matching words and definitions.

LESSON #136

Fill-in-the-Blank Questions

Estimated Time: 15 minutes

Fill-in-the-blank questions are another common type of test question you will see. A fill-in-the-blank question has a word missing in the sentence. You have to figure out the missing word that makes the sentence correct. Most of the time there is a word bank, or list of words, to choose from.

Here is an example of a fill-in-the-blank question.

WORD BANK		
Civil	French & Indian	Revolutionary

The _____ War was a war between England and the American colonies for America's Independence.

The first thing to do is to look at the words in the word bank. Think about each word and what you know about those words. Then, read the sentence. Where you see the blank, say *blank*. For this example, you would say, "The *blank* War was a war between England and the American colonies for America's Independence." Think about each of the choices in the word bank. See if you can narrow it down to a few choices. Put each choice into the blank and say it to yourself. Which choice sounds correct?

The correct answer for this example is *Revolutionary*. This was the war between England and the American colonies. Once you choose the correct answer, cross off the word in the word bank so you know you cannot chose that one again.

Throughout this week, you will practice fill-in-the-blank questions for each subject.

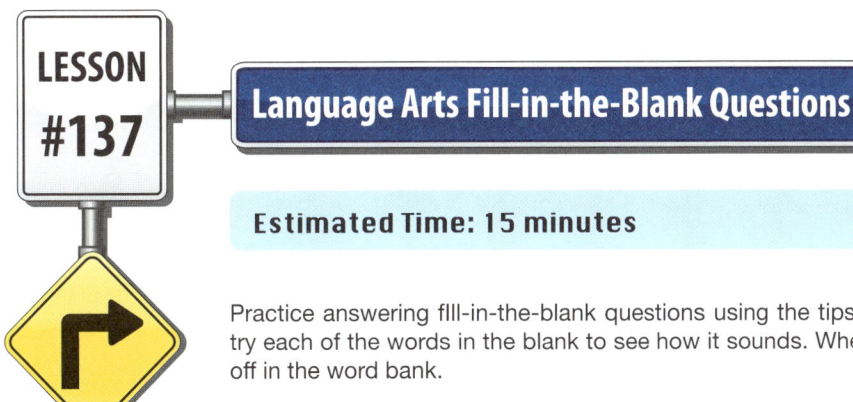

LESSON #137

Language Arts Fill-in-the-Blank Questions

Estimated Time: 15 minutes

Practice answering fill-in-the-blank questions using the tips you learned yesterday. Remember to try each of the words in the blank to see how it sounds. When you find the correct answer, cross it off in the word bank.

Turn to page 173 in Section Two and complete the fill-in-the-blank questions.

LESSON #138

Math Fill-in-the-Blank Questions

Estimated Time: 15 minutes

Today, you will practice answering fill-in-the-blank questions in math. If you need help remembering different tips and strategies, you may need to refer to the information from two lessons ago.

Turn to page 177 in Section Two to answer the fill-in-the-blank questions.

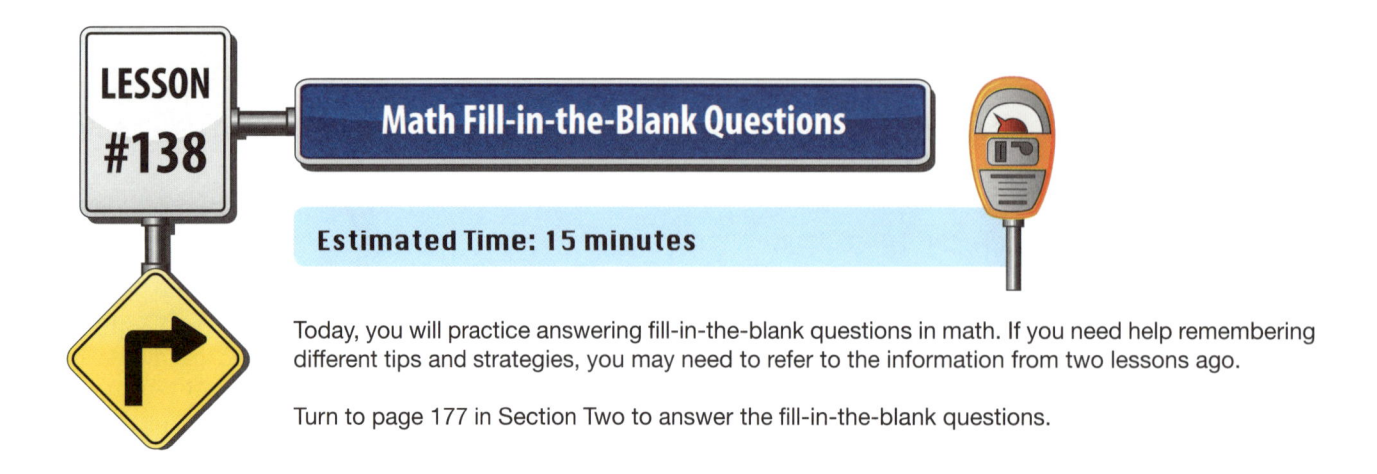

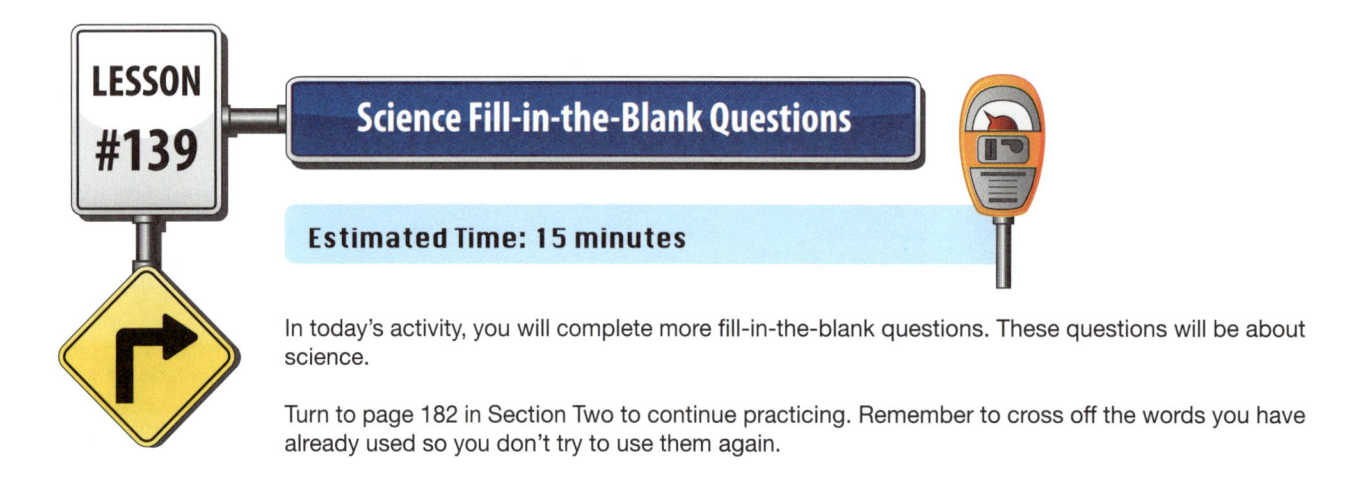

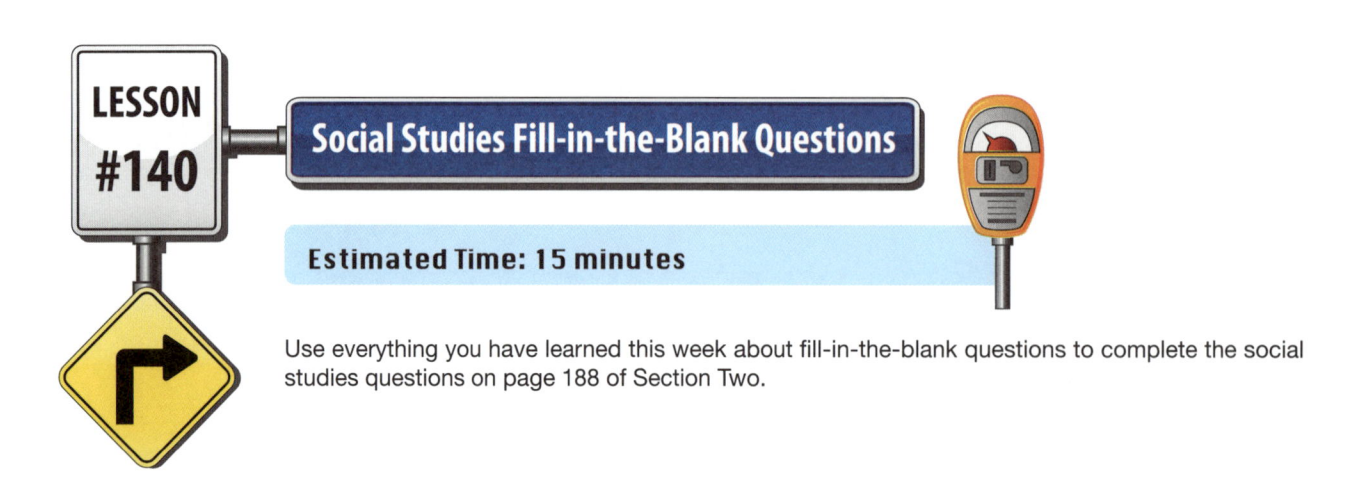

LESSON #139

Science Fill-in-the-Blank Questions

Estimated Time: 15 minutes

In today's activity, you will complete more fill-in-the-blank questions. These questions will be about science.

Turn to page 182 in Section Two to continue practicing. Remember to cross off the words you have already used so you don't try to use them again.

LESSON #140

Social Studies Fill-in-the-Blank Questions

Estimated Time: 15 minutes

Use everything you have learned this week about fill-in-the-blank questions to complete the social studies questions on page 188 of Section Two.

LESSON #141

Labeling Diagrams

Estimated Time: 15 minutes

Often, especially in science, you will use a diagram to help you learn about an idea or concept. A *diagram* is a picture of something with parts, like the human body, a plant, or the solar system, that is labeled. You may see diagrams in other subjects, but these are common to see in science.

This week, you will practice labeling diagrams. Diagrams are frequently on tests to see what you can remember about the parts of something.

Let's take a look at an example of a diagram.

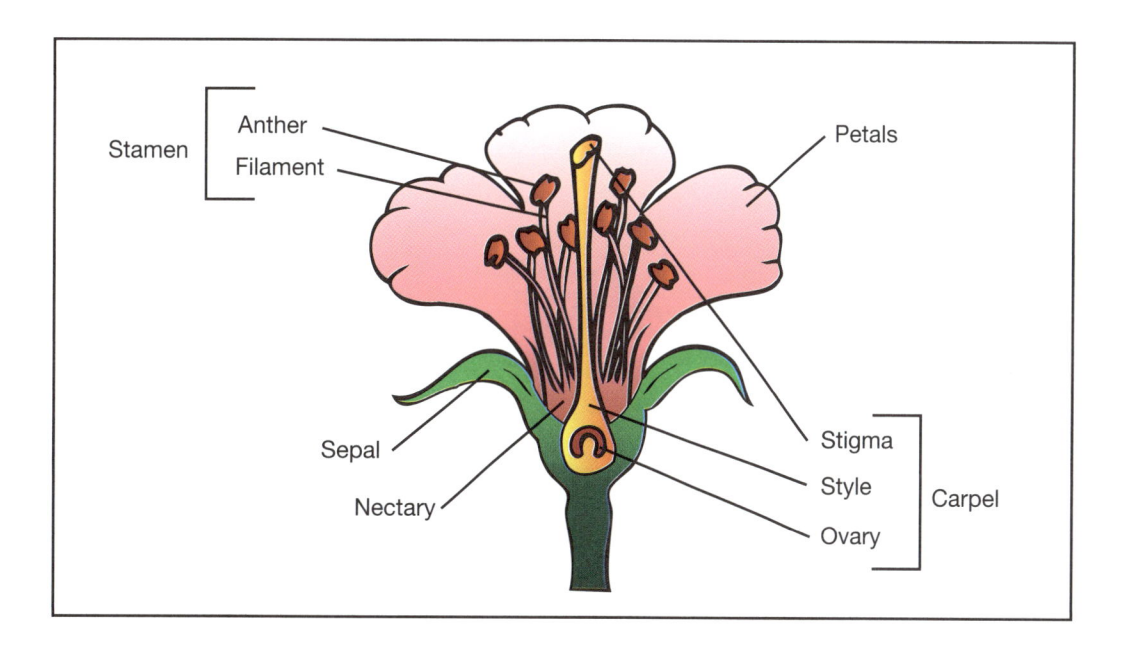

This is a diagram that shows the parts of a flower. It has a title so that you know what you are looking at. Each part of the flower has an arrow pointing to it with that part of the flower labeled. Diagrams help you to see what these parts look like, and they help you to remember each part. On a test, you may have to label a diagram. Each of the words will be removed from the diagram, and you will have to label each part. Sometimes there is a word box, other times there will not be. This week, you will practice labeling different diagrams.

Can you think of reasons why studying diagrams is helpful? _____
_____
_____
_____
_____

WEEK 29

LESSON #142

Labeling a Diagram

Estimated Time: 15 minutes

Today, you will practice labeling a diagram. The diagram you will label will have a word bank for you to choose from. When you label this diagram in Section Two, label the parts you already know. Cross them off the word bank so you know not to use them again. Then think about what you know about the topic to carefully label the rest of the diagram.

Before you complete the diagram in Section Two, take a look at it below. You may already be familiar with this topic. Look at each of the planets and try to remember the order. You may want to use a mnemonic device like *My Very Energetic Mother Just Served Us Nachos* to help you remember the order of the planets.

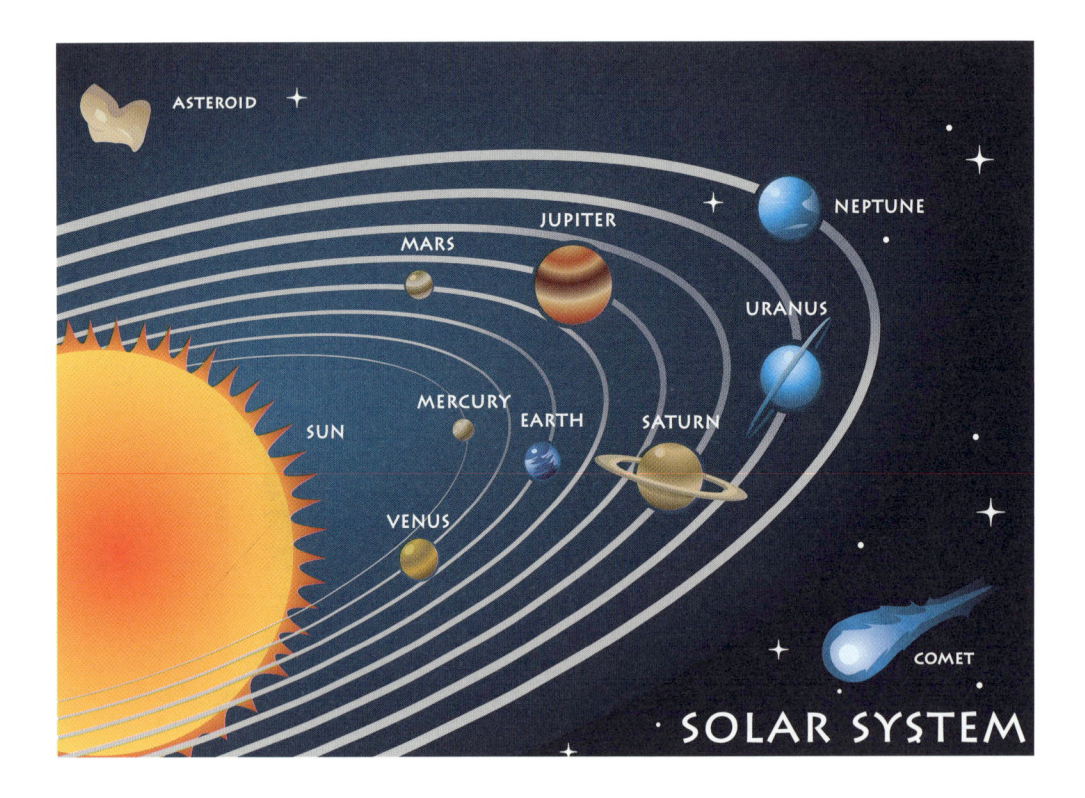

Now, turn to page 183 of Section Two to label this diagram.

LESSON #143

Labeling a Diagram

Estimated Time: 15 minutes

Yesterday, you practiced labeling a diagram using a word bank. Today, you will practice labeling a different diagram. Make sure to cross off each word as you use it in the word bank. This will help you make sure you don't use the word more than once. Review the diagram below.

When you are ready, turn to page 184 of Section Two and label the number for question 27.

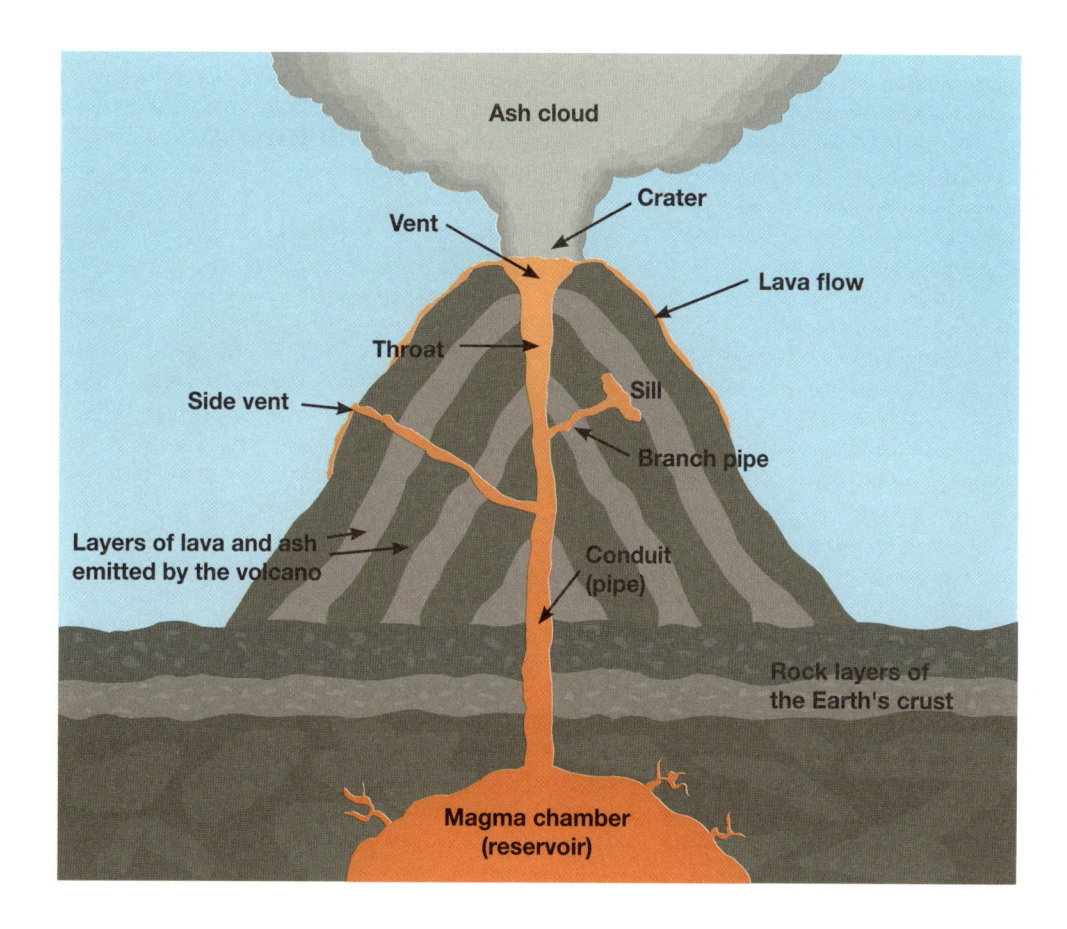

- Ash cloud
- Vent
- Crater
- Lava flow
- Throat
- Sill
- Side vent
- Branch pipe
- Layers of lava and ash emitted by the volcano
- Conduit (pipe)
- Rock layers of the Earth's crust
- Magma chamber (reservoir)

LESSON #144

Labeling a Diagram

Estimated Time: 15 minutes

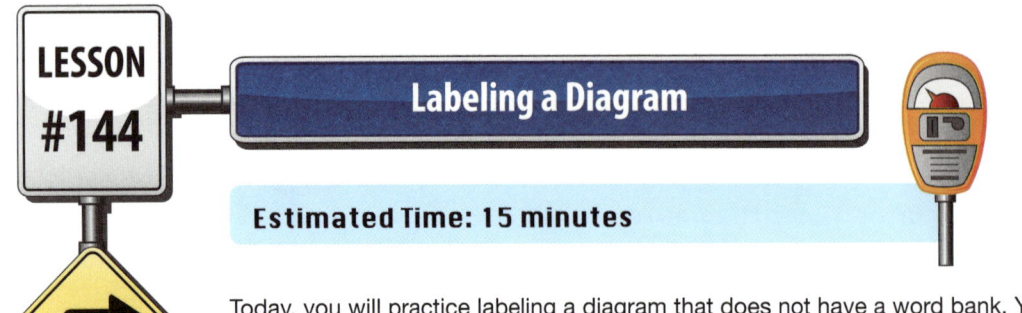

Today, you will practice labeling a diagram that does not have a word bank. You will see a diagram with arrows pointing to the parts you will need to name. Even though there is not a word bank given, you can create your own. In the margin of the paper, think of all of the words you know that could name the parts. Then, you can use these terms as your own word bank. Take a look at the diagram. Take a few moments to remember this.

Turn to page 185 in Section Two and complete the diagram labeled 28.

Earth's Interior

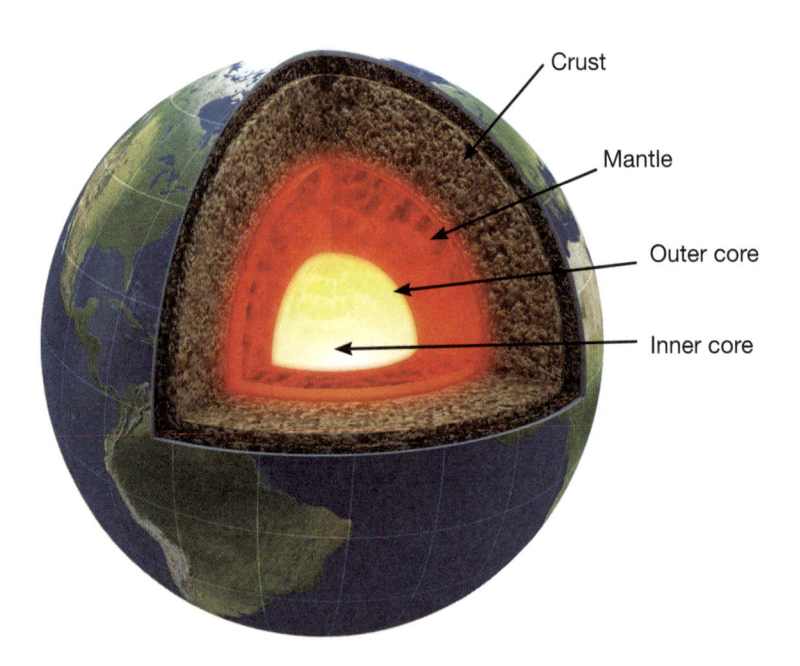

- Crust
- Mantle
- Outer core
- Inner core

LESSON #145

Social Studies Diagram

Estimated Time: 15 minutes

Diagrams can be used in subjects other than science. You may see diagrams used in social studies to show how a program or community works. Labeling a diagram in social studies is the same as labeling one in any other subject. You will need to choose the correct word from a word bank and label the part or picture. You have already learned about the three branches of government in social studies. Review the diagram below.

Turn to page 189 in Section Two and label the diagram.

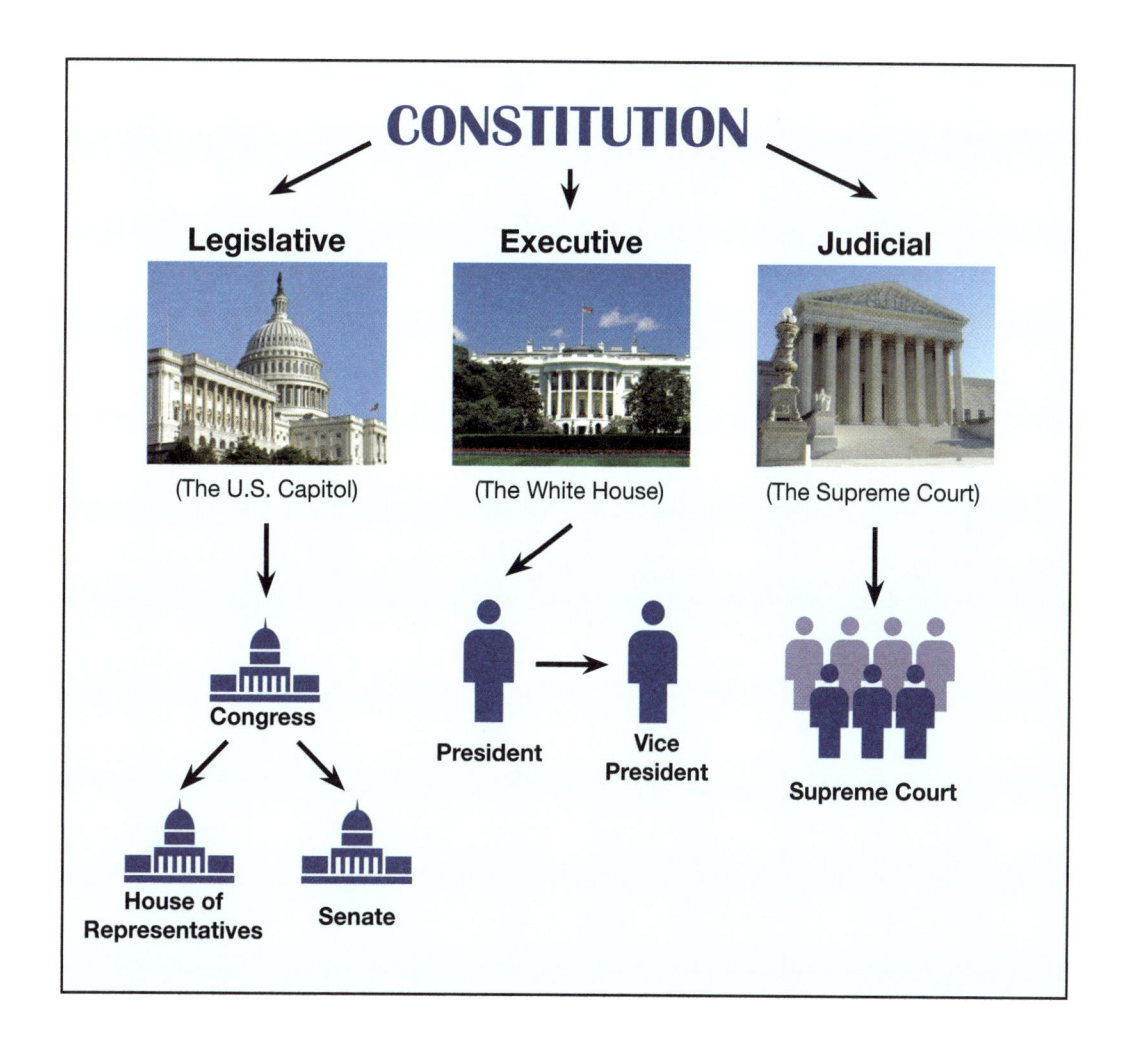

CONSTITUTION

Legislative — (The U.S. Capitol) → Congress → House of Representatives, Senate

Executive — (The White House) → President → Vice President

Judicial — (The Supreme Court) → Supreme Court

LESSON #146: Completing a Bar Graph

Estimated Time: 15 minutes

In math, you have already learned about different types of graphs. On tests, especially standardized tests, you will have to take data, and put it into a graph or chart. All week, you will practice doing this with different types of charts and graphs. Today you will review bar graphs and then make one of your own.

A bar graph is one way to show data in an organized way. Here is an example of what a bar graph looks like.

Jana's practice log:
Monday: 2 hours
Tuesday: 3 hours
Wednesday: 4 hours
Thursday: 1 hour
Friday: 2 hours

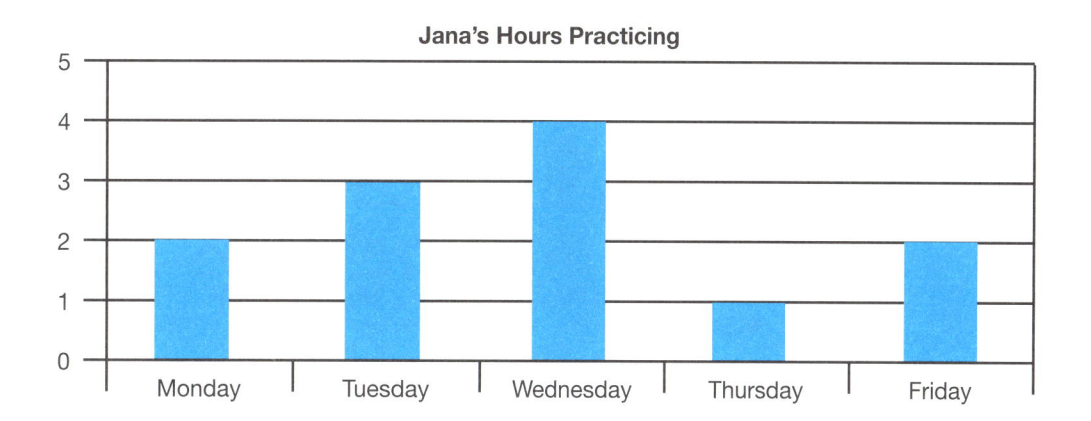

Jana's Hours Practicing

Day	Hours
Monday	2
Tuesday	3
Wednesday	4
Thursday	1
Friday	2

As you can see, this bar graph shows how many hours Jana practiced the piano each day. To make a chart like this, you will take the data you are given, and make a bar that high. For example, you can see Jana practiced for 2 hours on Monday, so the top of the bar goes up to the 2.

Turn to page 178 in Section Two to make a bar graph using the data you are given.

LESSON #147

Making a Pictograph

Estimated Time: 15 minutes

Another type of graph that displays information is a pictograph. This type of graph uses pictures to show how many of something. Take a look at the data and graph below.

Number of apples picked:
Karen: 5
Gina: 3
Maria: 4
Natalie: 4

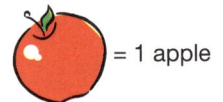

🍎 = 1 apple

Karen	🍎 🍎 🍎 🍎 🍎
Gina	🍎 🍎 🍎
Maria	🍎 🍎 🍎 🍎
Natalie	🍎 🍎 🍎 🍎

Each picture of an apple stands for one apple. You can see how Karen picked 5 apples and there are 5 apples in her row. Pictographs are an easy way to see data using pictures.

Turn to page 178 of Section Two and complete number 28.

LESSON #148

Completing a Tally Chart

Estimated Time: 15 minutes

A tally chart is a great way to keep track of a large number of things, such as scores in a game. Take a look at an example of the data and the chart below.

Tennis matches won:
Christina: 8
Michelle: 6

Christina	|||| |||
Michelle	||||	

For each point, make a mark called a tally. On the fifth tally, cross out the 4. That makes it easy to count the points because you can count by groups of five.

Turn to page 179 in Section Two and complete number 29 to practice making a tally chart.

LESSON #149

Using a Graph to Answer Questions

Estimated Time: 15 minutes

Many times on tests, there will be questions to answer about a graph or chart. Today and tomorrow, you will practice this. To do this, you will need to look carefully at the graph. Read each question, and then look to the graph to answer the question. Each answer must be labeled. Let's look at an example.

Tennis Matches Won

Christina	|||| |||
Michelle	||||	

DETOUR NEXT PAGE

END DETOUR How many more tennis matches did Christina win than Michelle?

To answer this question, you can figure out how many matches Christina won (8), and how many Michelle won (6). You know that *how many more than* means you will need to subtract.

$$8 - 6 = 2$$

Christina won 2 more matches than Michelle.

You can also look at the tallies and see that there are 2 more tally marks in Christina's column than Michelle's. Either way, you will get the same answer.

Turn to page 179 in Section Two and complete questions 30 – 33 in section I.

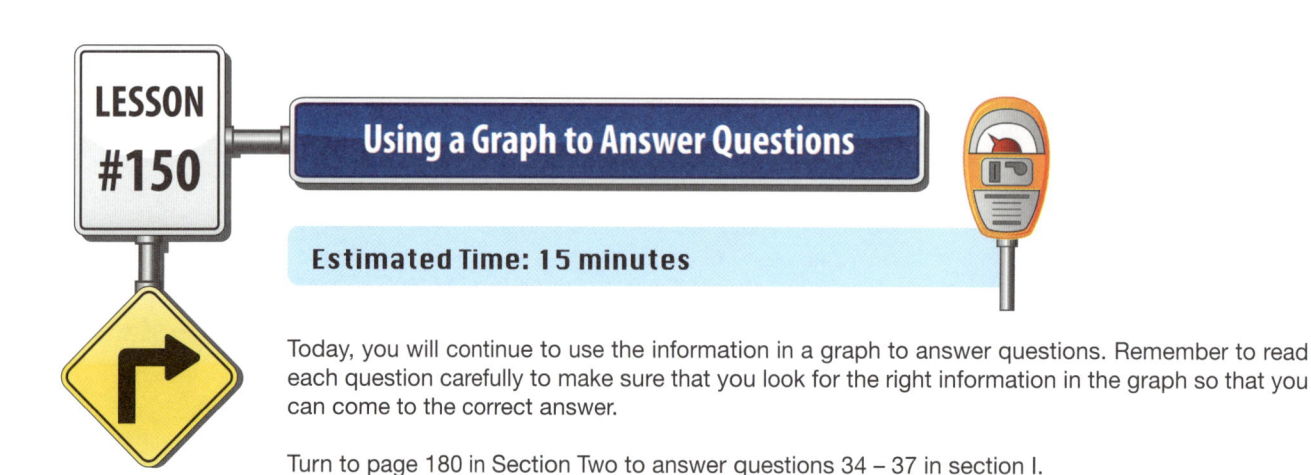

LESSON #150: Using a Graph to Answer Questions

Estimated Time: 15 minutes

Today, you will continue to use the information in a graph to answer questions. Remember to read each question carefully to make sure that you look for the right information in the graph so that you can come to the correct answer.

Turn to page 180 in Section Two to answer questions 34 – 37 in section I.

Lesson #151: What is a Rubric?

Estimated Time: 15 minutes

When writing a story or report that will be graded, how do you know what to write about? A rubric is a list of things that a good essay, composition, or report must contain. It tells you what your teacher will grade you on. A rubric will tell you how many points you will earn, and what you will need to do in order to earn the best score possible. Here is an example of what rubric might look like:

Focus:

_____ / 7 Web planner

Content:

_____ / 2 Good topic sentence
_____ / 6 Six supporting sentences (one for each box on the web planner)

Style:

_____ / 2 Complete and correct sentences
_____ / 2 Different types and lengths of sentences
_____ / 2 Consistent voice and tense
_____ / 2 Varied sentence beginnings

Conventions:

_____ / 1 Indented paragraph
_____ / 1 No mistakes with capitalization
_____ / 1 No mistakes with punctuation
_____ / 2 No mistakes with grammar
_____ / 1 No mistakes with spelling

Total:

_____ / 30

You can see the things you would be graded on. You can also see how many points each item is worth. For example, next to the item *Good topic sentence*, you can see that this is worth 2 points. If you include a good topic sentence in your final composition, you will earn 2 points. If you do not, then you will not earn those 2 points.

A rubric is like a checklist of things to make sure you have done in your composition or project. You can also see how many points each item is worth. After you have written your answer, you can use the rubric to estimate about how many points you think you have earned.

Later this week, you will look at examples of rubrics and how to use them to get the best score possible.

Give at least one reason why using a rubric when writing is a good idea: _____
_____
_____

LESSON #152

Using a Rubric to Write an Essay

Estimated Time: 15 minutes

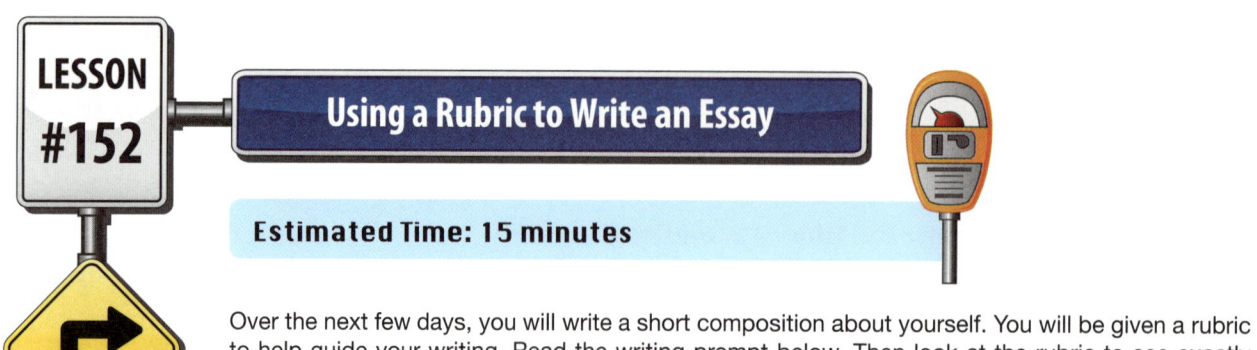

Over the next few days, you will write a short composition about yourself. You will be given a rubric to help guide your writing. Read the writing prompt below. Then look at the rubric to see exactly what your composition needs to include so you can earn the best score possible. As explained in the previous lesson, you can see that each item you must include in your paragraph is given a point value. If you explain why your family is special, you will earn 1 point. If you do not do this, then you will not earn the point. A rubric gives you hints on what you need to do to earn the best score possible.

Write one paragraph about your family and what makes your family special.

Grading Rubric

Score	Criteria
0 1 2	Good topic sentence
0 1 2 3 4 5	One paragraph of at least five sentences
0 1	Explains why family is special
0 1 2	Complete and correct sentences
0 1 2	Consistent verb tense
0 1 2	Different sentence beginnings
0 1	Indented paragraph
0 1	Uses capital letters correctly
0 1	Uses punctuation correctly
0 1 2	Uses grammar correctly
0 1	No spelling mistakes
_____/20	Total score

LESSON #153

Using Rubrics in a Writing Assignment

Estimated Time: 15 minutes

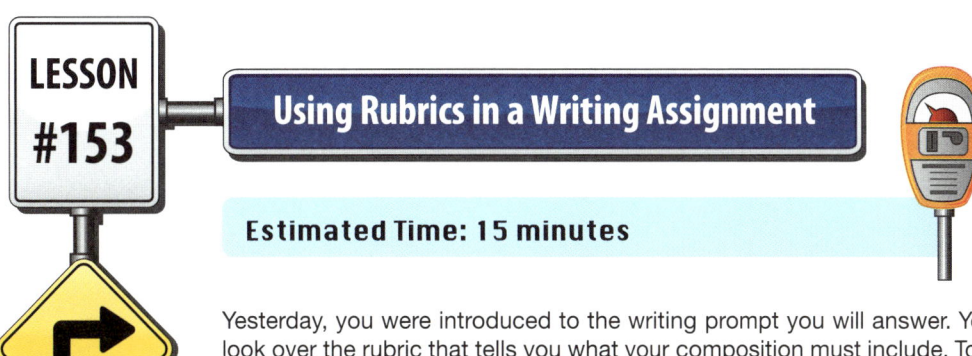

Yesterday, you were introduced to the writing prompt you will answer. You also had the chance to look over the rubric that tells you what your composition must include. Today, you will begin to plan out your composition. Think about what you want to say and what details and example you want to include in your paragraph. The rubric is below and tells you what you need to remember to include. Use this to help you begin to plan your paragraph. Use the space below to plan out your paragraph.

Grading Rubric

0 1 2	Good topic sentence
0 1 2 3 4 5	One paragraph of at least five sentences
0 1	Explains why family is special
0 1 2	Complete and correct sentences
0 1 2	Consistent verb tense
0 1 2	Different sentence beginnings
0 1	Indented paragraph
0 1	Uses capital letters correctly
0 1	Uses punctuation correctly
0 1 2	Uses grammar correctly
0 1	No spelling mistakes
____/20	Total score

Lesson #154

Using Rubrics in a Writing Assignment

Estimated Time: 15 minutes

In the last lesson, you began to plan out your paragraph about your family and why it is special. Today, you will write your paragraph. Make sure to follow the rubric.

_____
_____
_____
_____
_____
_____
_____
_____
_____
_____
_____

Grading Rubric

Score	Criteria
0 1 2	Good topic sentence
0 1 2 3 4 5	One paragraph of at least five sentences
0 1	Explains why family is special
0 1 2	Complete and correct sentences
0 1 2	Consistent verb tense
0 1 2	Different sentence beginnings
0 1	Indented paragraph
0 1	Uses capital letters correctly
0 1	Uses punctuation correctly
0 1 2	Uses grammar correctly
0 1	No spelling mistakes
____/20	Total score

LESSON #155

Using Rubrics in a Writing Assignment

Estimated Time: 15 minutes

Get out the paragraph you wrote about your family yesterday. Use the rubric below to grade your own assignment. Circle the amount of points you think you would earn. For example, if you are grading yourself on sentences in your paragraph, you can see that you must have at least five sentences. If you only have four sentences, then you should circle 4. If you have seven sentences, you can circle 5.

Read your paragraph and grade yourself using the rubric below.

Grading Rubric

0 1 2	Good topic sentence
0 1 2 3 4 5	One paragraph of at least five sentences
0 1	Explains why family is special
0 1 2	Complete and correct sentences
0 1 2	Consistent verb tense
0 1 2	Different sentence beginnings
0 1	Indented paragraph
0 1	Uses capital letters correctly
0 1	Uses punctuation correctly
0 1 2	Uses grammar correctly
0 1	No spelling mistakes
____/20	Total score

How many points did you earn? _____

Now that you have graded your own work, is there anything you should have done differently in your composition? _____
_____
_____
_____
_____
_____

LESSON #156

Writing a Science Open-Ended Response

Estimated Time: 15 minutes

You have already practiced writing open-ended responses in math and in reading. This type of question is also asked in science. Throughout this week, you will write a response to a science question.

Just like when you answered the open-ended questions in reading and math, it is important for you to read the directions and the question very carefully. Read it two times, or even three, if you need to, before beginning to answer the question.

Today, you will read the directions and the question. Tomorrow, you will begin to put your answer together.

Below is data collected from an area in California showing the six most recent earthquakes and their magnitudes.

Year of Earthquake	Magnitude
1954	4.6
1963	7.0
1974	4.0
1982	3.9
1992	8.4
1999	7.7

A. Using the data in the chart, make a hypothesis of when you think the next earthquake might strike. _____

   Give an explanation of why you think this way. _____
   _____
   _____

B. Make a hypothesis of whether you think the next earthquake will be weak or strong.
   Give an explanation of why you think this way. _____
   _____
   _____

C. Give one reason why earthquakes happen. _____
   _____
   _____

LESSON #157

Writing a Science Open-Ended Response

Estimated Time: 15 minutes

Yesterday, you read the open-ended question that you will answer this week. Today, you will complete the next step. Read the question and directions again. Underline what you will need to do so that when you write the answer you know what you will need to write about. Look at the question below. Underline the things you will need to do to answer the question.

Below is data collected from an area in California showing the six most recent earthquakes and their magnitudes.

Year of Earthquake	Magnitude
1954	4.6
1963	7.0
1974	4.0
1982	3.9
1992	8.4
1999	7.7

A. Using the data in the chart, make a hypothesis of when you think the next earthquake might strike. _____

   Give an explanation of why you think this way. _____
   _____
   _____

B. Make a hypothesis of whether you think the next earthquake will be weak or strong. Give an explanation of why you think this way. _____
   _____
   _____

C. Give one reason why earthquakes happen. _____
   _____
   _____

LESSON #158

Answering Science Open-Ended Questions

Estimated Time: 15 minutes

Today, you will begin to answer the open-ended question. You have already read it three times, and you should have underlined what you are supposed to do to correctly answer it. Answer section A. Make sure to complete both questions in the section. When you give an explanation, you must answer in complete sentences. Give at least two sentences to explain your answer.

Below is data collected from an area in California showing the six most recent earthquakes and their magnitudes.

Year of Earthquake	Magnitude
1954	4.6
1963	7.0
1974	4.0
1982	3.9
1992	8.4
1999	7.7

A. Using the data in the chart, make a hypothesis of when you think the next earthquake might strike. _____

Give an explanation of why you think this way. _____
_____
_____

B. Make a hypothesis of whether you think the next earthquake will be weak or strong.
Give an explanation of why you think this way. _____
_____
_____

C. Give one reason why earthquakes happen. _____
_____
_____

LESSON #159: Answering Science Open-Ended Questions

Estimated Time: 15 minutes

Today, you will continue to answer the open-ended question. You have already read the question multiple times, and you should have underlined what you are supposed to do to correctly answer it. Answer section B. Make sure to complete both questions in the section. When you give an explanation, you must answer in complete sentences. Give at least two sentences to explain your answer.

Year of Earthquake	Magnitude
1954	4.6
1963	7.0
1974	4.0
1982	3.9
1992	8.4
1999	7.7

A. Using the data in the chart, make a hypothesis of when you think the next earthquake might strike. _____

Give an explanation of why you think this way. _____
_____
_____

B. Make a hypothesis of whether you think the next earthquake will be weak or strong.
Give an explanation of why you think this way. _____
_____
_____

C. Give one reason why earthquakes happen. _____
_____
_____

LESSON #160

Answering Science Open-Ended Questions

Estimated Time: 15 minutes

Today, you will finish your answer to the open-ended question. You have already read the question multiple times, and you should have underlined what you are supposed to do to correctly answer it. Answer section C. When you give an explanation, you must answer in complete sentences. Give at least two sentences to explain your answer using evidence from the text.

Year of Earthquake	Magnitude
1954	4.6
1963	7.0
1974	4.0
1982	3.9
1992	8.4
1999	7.7

A. Using the data in the chart, make a hypothesis of when you think the next earthquake might strike. _____

Give an explanation of why you think this way. _____
_____
_____

B. Make a hypothesis of whether you think the next earthquake will be weak or strong.
Give an explanation of why you think this way. _____
_____
_____

C. Give one reason why earthquakes happen. _____
_____
_____

151

LESSON #161

Answering Social Studies Open-Ended Questions

Estimated Time: 15 minutes

In social studies, there will be times you may have to answer an open-ended question. This week you will answer a social studies question step-by-step. Just like when you answer this type of question in math, reading, or science, you will first read the question and the directions. You may need to read the question more than once to understand what it is asking.

Read the open-ended question and the directions below.

A. The United Stated government has three branches. List them below.
_____
_____
_____

B. Choose one of the three branches and tell what that branch is responsible for.
_____
_____
_____
_____
_____
_____

C. Think about the branch you chose. Why is this branch of the government important?
_____
_____
_____
_____
_____
_____

LESSON #162

Answering Social Studies Open-Ended Questions

Estimated Time: 15 minutes

The second step in answering an open-ended question is to underline each thing you will need to do to correctly respond to the question. Look for the verbs, like *explain*, *list*, or *describe*. Tomorrow, you will begin to answer the first part of the question.

A. The United Stated government has three branches. List them below.
___
___
___

B. Choose one of the three branches and tell what that branch is responsible for.
___
___
___
___
___
___

C. Think about the branch you chose. Why is this branch of the government important?
___
___
___
___
___
___

LESSON #163

Answering Social Studies Open-Ended Questions

Estimated Time: 15 minutes

Today, you will begin to answer the open-ended question. Read the entire question once more. Answer only question A today. Remember to keep your answer within the response box. Anything written outside of the response box will not be graded. Tomorrow, you will answer question B.

A. The United Stated government has three branches. List them below.
___
___
___

B. Choose one of the three branches and tell what that branch is responsible for.
___
___
___
___
___
___

C. Think about the branch you chose. Why is this branch of the government important?
___
___
___
___
___
___

LESSON #164

Answering Social Studies Open-Ended Questions

Estimated Time: 15 minutes

Today, you will continue to answer the open-ended question. Read the entire question once more. Answer only question B today. Review your answer to question A to revisit what you were thinking. Your answer should include at least three sentences. Remember to keep your answer within the response box. Anything written outside of the response box will not be graded. Tomorrow, you will answer question C.

A. The United Stated government has three branches. List them below.
___
___
___

B. Choose one of the three branches and tell what that branch is responsible for.
___
___
___
___
___
___
___

C. Think about the branch you chose. Why is this branch of the government important?
___
___
___
___
___
___
___

LESSON #165

Answering Social Studies Open-Ended Questions

Estimated Time: 15 minutes

Today, you will continue to answer the open-ended question. Read the entire question once more. Answer only question C today. Your answer should include at least three sentences. Remember to keep your answer within the response box. Anything written outside of the response box will not be graded. When you are finished, go back and read your answer. If you see anything wrong, correct it.

A. The United Stated government has three branches. List them below.
_____
_____
_____

B. Choose one of the three branches and tell what that branch is responsible for.
_____
_____
_____
_____
_____
_____

C. Think about the branch you chose. Why is this branch of the government important?
_____
_____
_____
_____
_____
_____

157

LESSON #166

Essay Questions

Estimated Time: 10 minutes

You are already familiar with open-ended questions that you may see on a standardized test. A similar type of test question that you may see on a regular test is called an essay. You can answer an essay in any subject. The answer to an essay question will require you to think about an answer and write a response. An essay question should be written in paragraph form and in complete sentences. It also must answer the entire question using correct spelling, proper capitalization, and punctuation.

This week, you will practice writing a response to an essay question. This is very similar to writing a response to an open-ended question.

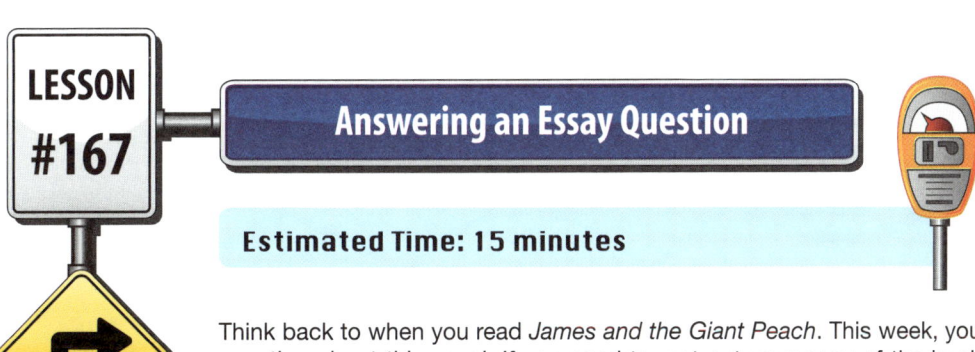

LESSON #167

Answering an Essay Question

Estimated Time: 15 minutes

Think back to when you read *James and the Giant Peach*. This week, you will respond to an essay question about this novel. If you need to, get out your copy of the book and review some of the main ideas.

Sometimes an essay question will ask your thoughts or opinions about a topic. Sometimes, an essay only wants facts. You will have to carefully read the question to make sure you answer in the correct way.

Below, you will find an essay question that pertains to *James and the Giant Peach*. Read the question and begin to brainstorm an answer. You can write some ideas on a piece of scratch paper, or you can make a graphic organizer. Do not begin to write your actual answer; you will do this later in the week.

Throughout *James and the Giant Peach*, James sees "strange and peculiar" things. Describe something strange and peculiar you have seen. Explain what makes this thing or event strange and peculiar.

LESSON #168

Answering an Essay Question

Estimated Time: 15 minutes

In the previous lesson, you were given an essay question from *James and the Giant Peach* to think about. Today, you will begin to plan out your essay.

Read the essay question again:
Throughout *James and the Giant Peach*, James sees "strange and peculiar" things. Describe something strange and peculiar you have seen. Explain what makes this thing or event strange and peculiar.

If you started to jot down some ideas and brainstorm yesterday, take out that sheet. If you did not, then you will need a sheet of paper to get your ideas flowing today.

Make a web to help you brainstorm an idea to answer this question. In the middle of your paper, draw a circle and write *strange and peculiar* in the middle. As you think of strange and peculiar things, draw a line coming off the circle in the middle and draw another circle at the end of the line. Write an idea in the new circle. As you think of new things, draw a new circle. As you think of details, add more bubbles. Do this for a few moments until you have decided what to write about.

Here is an example of what this type of web might look like as you begin:

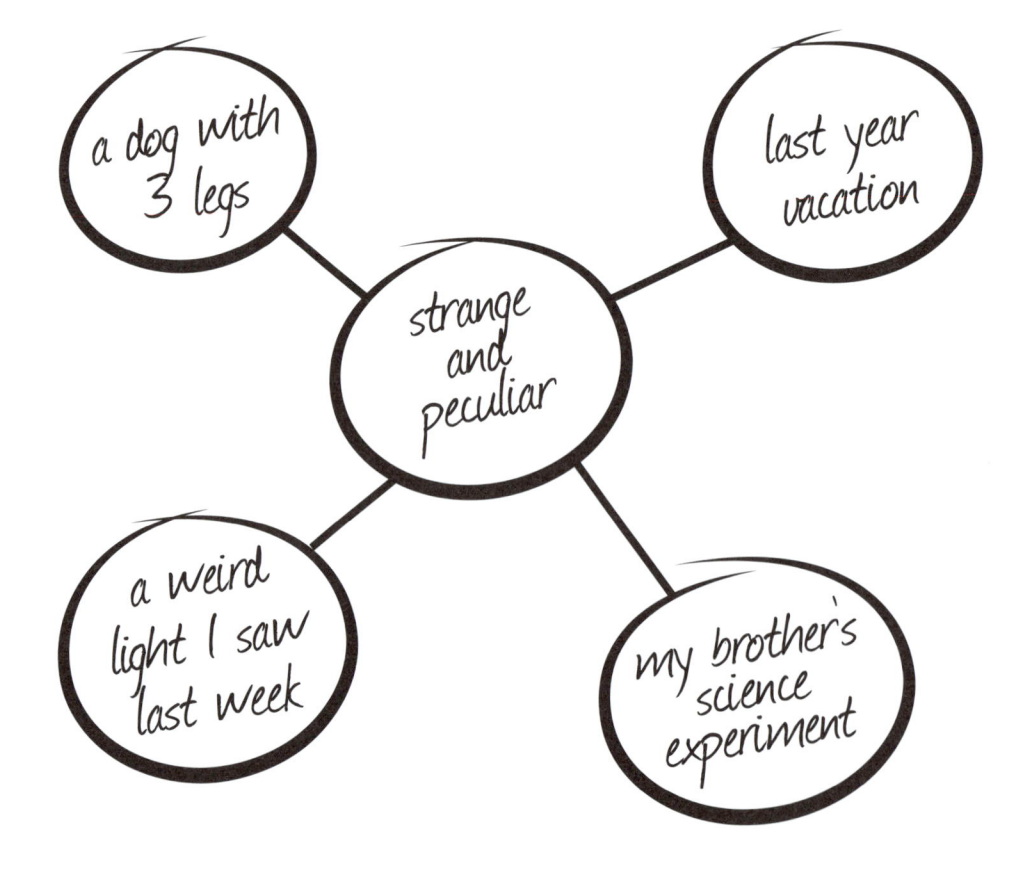

LESSON #169

Answering an Essay Question

Estimated Time: 15 minutes

Yesterday, you brainstormed an idea for the essay question you were given. Today, you will write your essay answer. For this question, you will want to give as much detail as you can. Try to make the reader feel like he or she is there with you by using describing words and phrases. Describing words and phrases may tell how big, what color, or what something smells like. For this essay, you should aim to write one or two paragraphs.

Throughout *James and the Giant Peach*, James sees "strange and peculiar" things. Describe something strange and peculiar you have seen. Explain what makes this thing or event strange and peculiar.

___
___
___
___
___
___
___
___
___
___
___
___
___
___
___
___
___
___
___
___

Lesson #170: Answering an Essay Question

Estimated Time: 15 minutes

Yesterday, you wrote your answer to the essay question about *James and the Giant Peach*. The last step before completing an essay is to read your answer and then look back at the question. Did you answer everything that was asked? Did you tell about a strange and peculiar event? Did you explain what made this event strange and peculiar? Did you use describing words? Did you spell the words correctly and use capital letters and proper punctuation? Go back and look at your answer to see if you did all of this. If you find any mistakes or errors, make sure to correct them.

WEEK 35

LESSON #171: I Got My Test Back! Now What?

Estimated Time: 15 minutes

Once you have taken a test and turned it in to your teacher, you are probably anxious to see your grade. Once you get your test back, what do you do? You probably look to see how you did. Hopefully, you have earned a good grade. You may have missed a few questions. When you get a test back and you have missed questions, you should review your mistakes so you learn the information. Sometimes, silly mistakes are made due to not reading the question carefully or to rushing through the test. This week, you will learn what to do once you get a test back so that you can always do your best on every test.

LESSON #172: I Got My Test Back! Now What?

Estimated Time: 15 minutes

No one is perfect, so there will be times when you miss questions on a test. There are ways that you can try to eliminate making mistakes.

When you get a test or a quiz back, take a few moments to see if you missed any questions. If you missed even just one question, look to see which one you missed. Find one of your most recent tests. Make a mark next to each missed question. You could also highlight the number of the question to help it stand out. This will make it easier for you to review your mistakes.

Tomorrow, you will look at why you may have made a mistake and what you can do to avoid making mistakes in the future.

LESSON #173: I Got My Test Back! Now What?

Estimated Time: 15 minutes

Once you get a test back, you should not just put it off to the side and forget about it. You can learn from your mistakes so that you don't make them again. Once you have figured out which questions you missed, think about why you missed them. Did you not read the directions carefully? If it was a math problem, did you add instead of subtract? Did you make a simple error? If it was an essay question, did you not give enough information? Or, did you just plain not understand what to do?

Take a look at the test you looked at yesterday. Look at each of the questions you missed. With your Guide, decide why you missed that particular question. Next to that problem, make a quick note about why that problem was wrong. This can help you to figure out how not to make the mistake again.

LESSON #174: I Got My Test Back! Now What?

Estimated Time: 15 minutes

Over the past two days, you looked at an old test and found the problems or questions you missed. Yesterday, you took some time with your Guide to figure out why you missed those questions. Today, you will solve the problem again, look up the correct answer, or redo the question. You should refer back to your textbook for help with looking up the information.

If you did not read or follow the directions carefully, go back and read them again and underline what you did wrong. The next time you take a test, you will know to take your time reading the directions.

Look at the rest of the questions you missed on your test and find the correct answers.

LESSON #175

I Got My Test Back! Now What?

Estimated Time: 15 minutes

Now that you have reviewed a recent test and have seen what you did wrong and why you did it, think about ways you can make sure to not make these mistakes again.

List things you can do to eliminate as many errors as possible when taking a test (add more lines if you need to):

- _____
- _____
- _____
- _____
- _____
- _____
- _____
- _____

WEEK 36

LESSON #176

Putting It All Together

Estimated Time: 15 minutes

You have come to the final week of third grade! Throughout this year, you have learned many tips, techniques, strategies, and skills to help you become a great student and good test taker. You will put everything you have learned this year to the test. Each day, you will complete a few test questions in a final practice test. Each section will use a variety of different test questions. Think hard and take your time and you will do well.

Turn to page 191 of Section Two (final practice test) and complete section A.

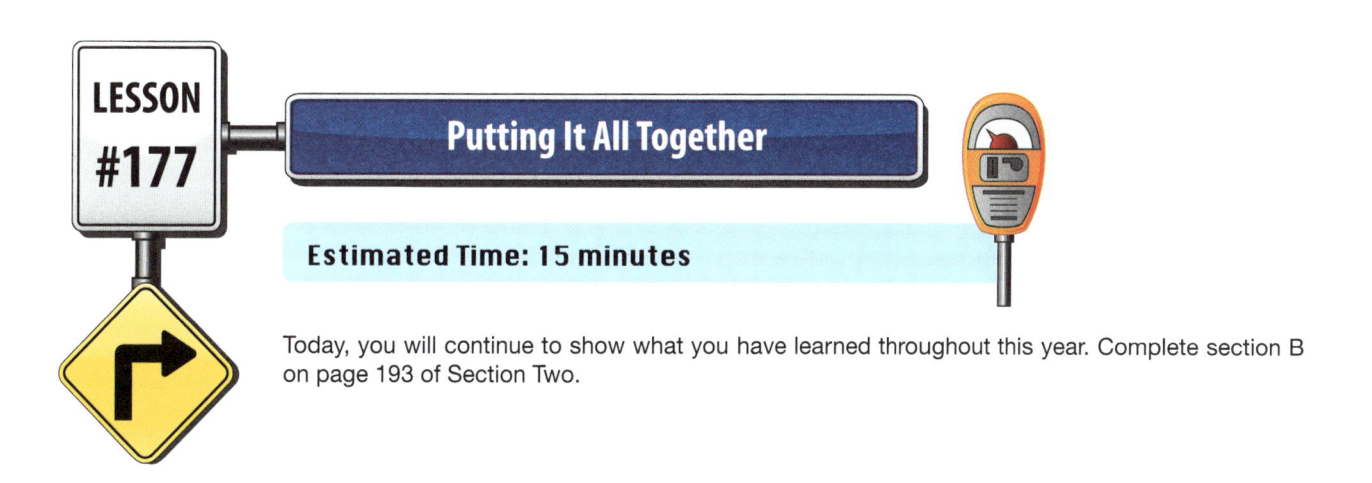

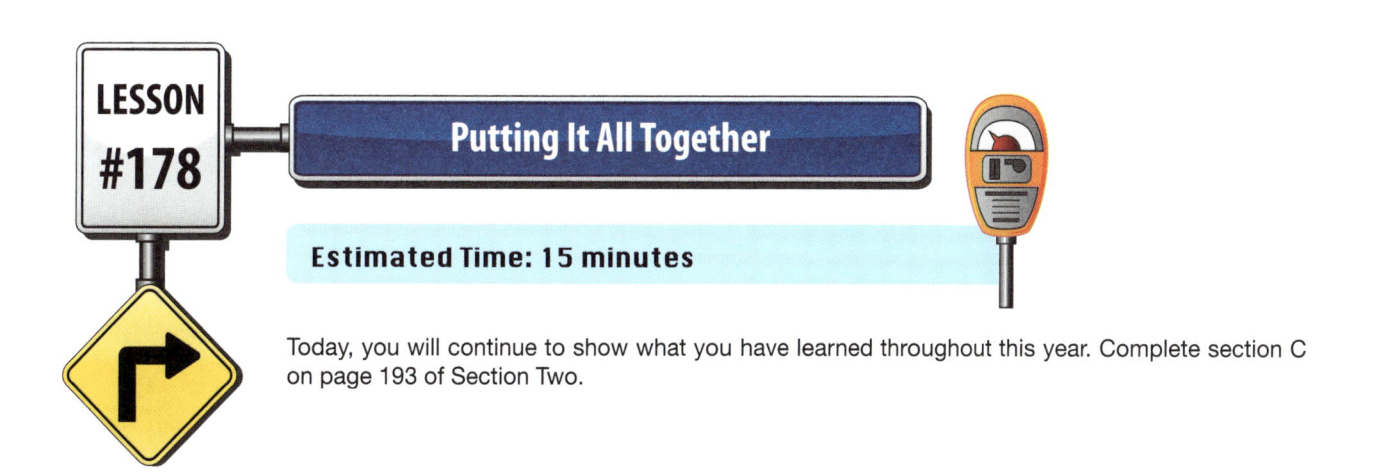

LESSON #177

Putting It All Together

Estimated Time: 15 minutes

Today, you will continue to show what you have learned throughout this year. Complete section B on page 193 of Section Two.

LESSON #178

Putting It All Together

Estimated Time: 15 minutes

Today, you will continue to show what you have learned throughout this year. Complete section C on page 193 of Section Two.

LESSON #179

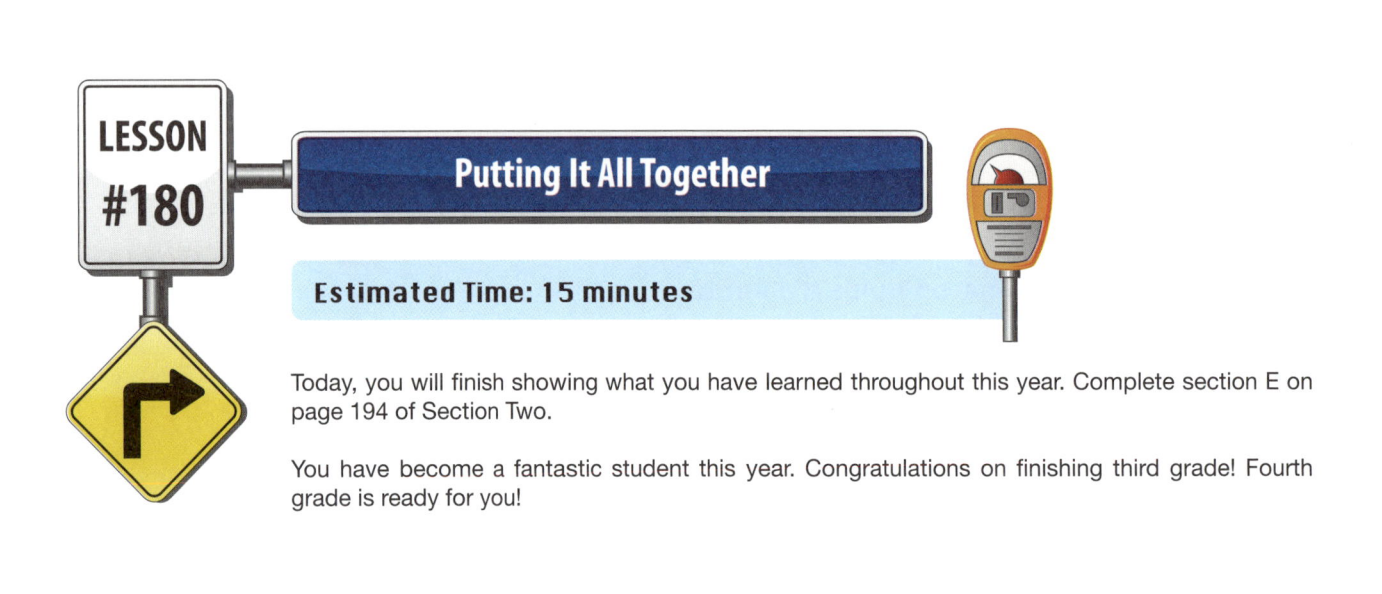

Putting It All Together

Estimated Time: 15 minutes

Today, you will continue to show what you have learned throughout this year. Complete section D on page 193 of Section Two.

LESSON #180

Putting It All Together

Estimated Time: 15 minutes

Today, you will finish showing what you have learned throughout this year. Complete section E on page 194 of Section Two.

You have become a fantastic student this year. Congratulations on finishing third grade! Fourth grade is ready for you!

STOP

END OF SECTION ONE

SECTION TWO

PRACTICE

PRACTICE TEST #1
LANGUAGE ARTS

A. Multiple Choice Questions
Read the questions you will need to answer first. Then, read the passage. As you realize answers are wrong, cross them off. Circle the correct answer.

There are nearly sixty national parks in the United States. The US government cares for these areas. The government has written many special laws to help. These laws keep the land safe. They guard the animals that live there. The national parks are known for many reasons. They have incredible wildlife and pretty landscapes. They offer a range of outdoor activities. Millions of tourists visit them each year. They come from all parts of the world. Two of the most popular parks to see are Hawaii Volcanoes and Rocky Mountain National Parks. This splendid pair has many similarities and differences.

Hawaii Volcanoes and Rocky Mountain National Parks are similar in many ways. Both are open every day of the year. They became national parks in the early 1900s. Each has a gorgeous view. They offer a variety of fun activities, like hiking and horseback riding. Each place is perfect to relax. They are also both known for their unpredictable weather. Either place can be cold and rainy on any given day. It is best to wear layers of clothing. This way you are ready for all weather. Both of these parks are partly created with igneous rock. Igneous rock forms when hot lava cools.

These two parks also have key differences. One is a group of volcanoes. The other is a mountain range. They are found in very different locations. Hawaii Volcanoes stands on the southern part of Hawaii, also known as the Big Island. There you will find two of the world's most active volcanoes. Rocky Mountain National Park is in northern Colorado. It is one of the longest mountain ranges in the world. The parks were shaped in different ways. Over millions of years the lava from the volcanoes formed the shape of the Hawaiian island. The Rocky Mountains were slowly shaped by glaciers and rivers. Hawaii Volcanoes has less extreme weather than Rocky Mountain National Park. In Hawaii Volcanoes, the temperature stays between fifty and seventy degrees for most of the year. At Rocky Mountain, it can range from below zero to the upper eighties. The animals found at each park are quite different. Hawaii is home to many rare birds. You may also see an endangered sea turtle. In the Rocky Mountains, many animals have thick fur. They need it to keep warm in the cold weather. Some examples are elks, moose, bears, and bighorn sheep.

1. Who takes care of United States National Parks?
   A. people in the community
   B. park rangers
   C. the US government
   D. no one

2. Which of the following is a similarity of Hawaiian volcanoes and Rocky Mountain National Park?
   A. They have the same kinds of animals.
   B. They both have unpredictable weather.
   C. They both have lava eruptions.
   D. The parks are shaped in the same geological ways.

3. Which of the following is a fact?
   A. Rocky Mountain National Park is in northern Colorado.
   B. Hawaii is the most beautiful place in the world.
   C. The animals that live at Rocky Mountain National Park are very cute.
   D. A trip to Colorado would be the best trip ever.

4. What is the author's purpose for writing this article?
   A. To suggest a location for vacation.
   B. To explain the types of animals that live in Hawaii and Colorado.
   C. To tell the similarities and differences between two different locations.
   D. To discuss why Colorado is better than Hawaii.

171

PRACTICE TEST #1

B. Using Context Clues
Read each sentence. Use context clues to help you choose the correct meaning of the underlined word.

5. She was an ordinary young girl, but she had grown bored with her common life.
   A. famous
   B. normal
   C. extraordinary
   D. silly

6. Jasmine was grateful for the help.
   A. unhappy
   B. jealous
   C. rude
   D. thankful

7. She had heard a shy girl with a stunning voice, singing the most beautiful song.
   A. ugly
   B. invisible
   C. very pretty
   D. strange

8. But Midas had one flaw, one weakness in his character. He often made decisions quickly, without thinking about what the outcome might be.
   A. imperfection
   B. strength
   C. bizarre
   D. friend

C. True or False Questions
Read each statement. If it is correct, write *T* for true on the line. If it is incorrect, write *F* for false on the line.

9. _____ A sentence always has ending punctuation.

10. _____ Nouns describe actions.

11. _____ An exclamatory sentence always asks a question.

12. _____ Verbs tell the action in a sentence.

13. _____ A proper noun must start with a capital letter.

PRACTICE TEST #1

D. Matching
Match the vocabulary word to its definition.

_____ 14. curiosity   A. a person that helps or assists
_____ 15. mature   B. to have a discussion to come to an agreement
_____ 16. aide   C. a dog of many breeds
_____ 17. elderly   D. a desire to learn
_____ 18. mutt   E. to go after and retrieve
_____ 19. negotiate   F. to obey
_____ 20. fetch   G. grown up
_____ 21. obedient   H. an old person

E. Fill in the Blank
Fill in each blank with the correct word.

WORD BANK				
Wilbur	Charlotte	Fern	Avery	Templeton

22. Wilbur is saved from death by _____, who takes care of him like a baby.
23. The main character in *Charlotte's Web* is _____, who Charlotte describes as "Some Pig."
24. _____ is Fern's loud and rude brother.
25. The spider who writes in her web, and becomes Wilbur's friend is _____.
26. _____ is a rat that loves to eat and steal things.

PRACTICE TEST #2

MATH

A. Multiple Choice Questions
Choose and circle the best answer.

1. 211 + 45 =
    - A. 661
    - B. 256
    - C. 175
    - D. 265

2. Name this shape.

    - A. square
    - B. trapezoid
    - C. rhomboid
    - D. rectangle

3. How many tens are in the following number?

    4,893

    - A. 3
    - B. 9
    - C. 8
    - D. 4

4. Complete the number pattern. What are the next three numbers?

    0, 3, 6, 9, ___, ____, ____

    - A. 12, 15, 18
    - B. 18, 36, 72
    - C. 11, 13, 15
    - D. 10, 13, 16

B. Using Context Clues
Read each word problem. Underline the keyword and decide whether you need to add or subtract. Then solve the problem. Don't forget to label your answer!

5. Rebecca has 14 fuzzy stickers. She also has 7 puffy stickers. How many more fuzzy stickers does she have than puffy stickers?

175

PRACTICE TEST #2

6. John and Matthew collect toy cars. John has 10 blue cars and Matthew has 9 red cars. How many cars in all do the two boys have?

7. Jahleesa has 13 chocolate covered raisins. She ate 7. How many are left?

8. Jason read 3 books last week and 8 books this week. How many books in all has he read over the past two weeks?

C. Solving Word Problems
Circle the numbers you need to solve the problem. Underline the keywords. Solve and label your answer.

9. Rosa and her family are on vacation for two weeks. Rosa's mom has asked Rosa to take pictures of their trip. In the first week, Rosa took 87 pictures. In the second week, she took 132 pictures. How many pictures did she take of their family vacation in all?

10. Evan bought a bag of lollipops. There are 50 lollipops in the bag. He handed out 32 lollipops. How many does he have left?

D. Solving a Math Open-Ended Problem
Read the math problem below. Make sure to solve the problem and fully answer the question.

11. Holly is hungry for a snack. She decides she wants to buy a bag of pretzels. They cost 80¢. What combination of coins could Holly use to buy the pretzels? Show your work or explain your answer.

PRACTICE TEST #2

E. True or False Questions.
Read each statement or problem. If it is true, write *T* on the line. If it is false, write *F* on the line.

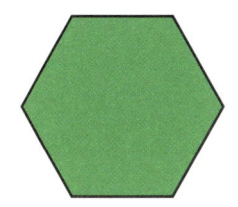

12. _____ This shape is a pentagon.
13. _____ The number underlined is in the thousands column. 8,310
14. _____ 9 x 3 = 27
15. _____ In a subtraction problem, difference means the answer.

F. Matching
Match each word to its definition.

_____ 16. cents   A. five cents
_____ 17. dollars   B. value in which bills are measured
_____ 18. penny   C. twenty-five cents
_____ 19. nickel   D. value in which coins are measured
_____ 20. dime   E. one cent
_____ 21. quarter   F. ten cents

G. Fill in the Blank
Read each statement. Choose the best answer from the word bank to complete the statement.

WORD BANK
ones   tens   hundreds   thousands   ten thousands

22. The underlined number is in the _____ column. 3̲25
23. The underlined number is in the _____ column. 1̲2,900
24. The underlined number is in the _____ column. 82̲1
25. The underlined number is in the _____ column. 7̲9,140
26. The underlined number is in the _____ column. 5,10̲3

PRACTICE TEST #2

H. Charts and Graphs

27. Use the data below to make a bar graph.

Marc's Study Time:

Monday:	3 hours
Tuesday:	2 hours
Wednesday:	2 hours
Thursday:	4 hours
Friday:	1 hour

Title _____

Hours

Days of the Week

28. Use the data below to make a pictograph.

Books read:
Steve: 3
Joe: 6
Michael: 2
Brandon: 4

Title _____

= _____ book

29. Use the data to complete the tally chart.

In a survey, kids were asked to choose their favorite drink from the following choices: milk, water, lemonade, and chocolate milk. Their responses are below. Put their answers into a tally chart.

Milk: 9
Water: 6
Lemonade: 7
Chocolate milk: 10

Title _____

Milk	
Water	
Lemonade	
Chocolate Milk	

I. Using Graphs to Answer Questions

Students were surveyed about their favorite season. Their answers have been recorded in the bar graph below. Use the graph to answer the questions.

Student's Favorite Seasons

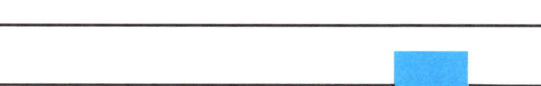

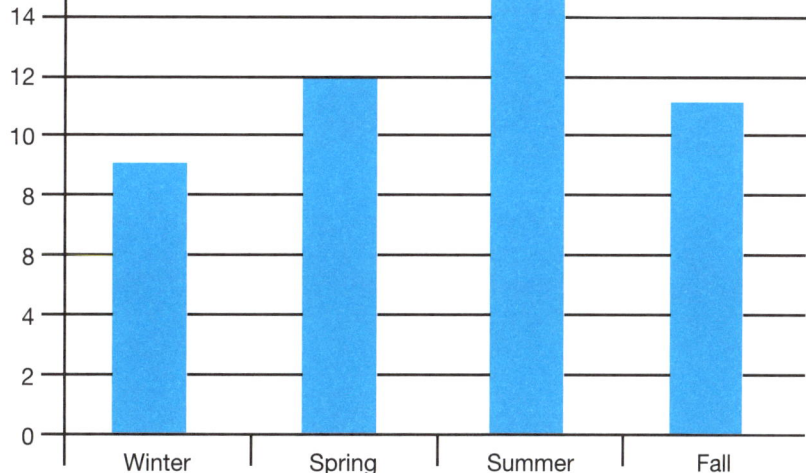

30. How many students like spring as their favorite season? _____

31. Which is the favorite season among students? _____

32. Which is the least favorite season among students? _____

33. How many more students like summer than fall? _____

PRACTICE TEST #2

Students were surveyed about their favorite school subject. Use the data in the pictograph to answer the questions below.

Favorite School Subjects

Reading	✏️✏️✏️✏️✏️
Math	✏️✏️✏️✏️✏️✏️
Science	✏️✏️✏️✏️
Social Studies	✏️✏️✏️

✏️ = 1 student

34. Which subject is the most popular? _____

35. How many students combined like science and social studies? _____

36. Which subject is the least popular? _____

37. How many more students like reading than social studies? _____

PRACTICE TEST #3

SCIENCE

A. Multiple Choice Questions
Choose and circle the best answer.

1. Which type of rock is formed by lava that has cooled?
    A. igneous
    B. metamorphic
    C. sedimentary
    D. all of the above

2. Which type of soil is best for growing plants?
    A. clay
    B. humus
    C. silt
    D. soil

3. Which of the following is NOT a layer of the Earth?
    A. crust
    B. plates
    C. mantle
    D. core

4. What is the correct term for air masses meeting?
    A. temperature
    B. humidity
    C. front
    D. all of the above

B. Vocabulary
Read each science term. Use what you know about other words to guess what this work might mean. Circle your answer.

5. revolution
    A. volume
    B. turning
    C. sound
    D. speed

6. prehistoric
    A. very new
    B. history
    C. very old
    D. before

7. sedimentary
    A. rock formed from sediments and pieces of other rock
    B. rock formed from sitting a long time
    C. rock formed from changing rock
    D. rock formed from fire

181

PRACTICE TEST #3

8. metamorphic
    A. rock formed from sediments and pieces of other rock
    B. rock formed from sitting a long time
    C. rock formed from changing rock
    D. rock formed from fire

C. True or False Questions
Read each statement. If the statement is true, write *T* on the line. If the statement is false, write *F* on the line.

9. ____ Without energy sound does not exist.
10. ____ Sound is created by air standing still.
11. ____ Vibrations create waves, and the waves become wind.
12. ____ You can hear sound with your eardrums.

D. Matching
Match the vocabulary word to its definition.

____ 13. observation   A. an educated guess
____ 14. hypothesis   B. a material found in nature and has never been alive
____ 15. crystal   C. things that change
____ 16. variables   D. the result of watching something carefully
____ 17. classify   E. a test used to determine the color of a rock or mineral
____ 18. streak   F. the shine or dullness of a rock or mineral
____ 19. luster   G. a way of organizing things based on its properties
____ 20. mineral   H. an organized group of molecules

E. Fill in the Blank
Read each statement. Choose the correct word from the word bank to complete the sentence.

WORD BANK

weather   temperature   precipitation   metorologist   humidity

21. Another name for rain, snow, sleet, and hail is _____.
22. A _____ is a scientist that studies the weather.
23. The measure of how hot or cold it is also known as _____.
24. The _____ is the condition of the air at a given time and place.
25. The amount of moisture in the air determines the _____.

F. Labeling Diagrams

26. Look at the diagram of the solar system. Use the words in the word bank to help you correctly name each part.

WORD BANK					
sun	Jupiter	Neptune	Mecury	comet	Mars
Earth	Venus	asteroid	Saturn	Uranus	moon

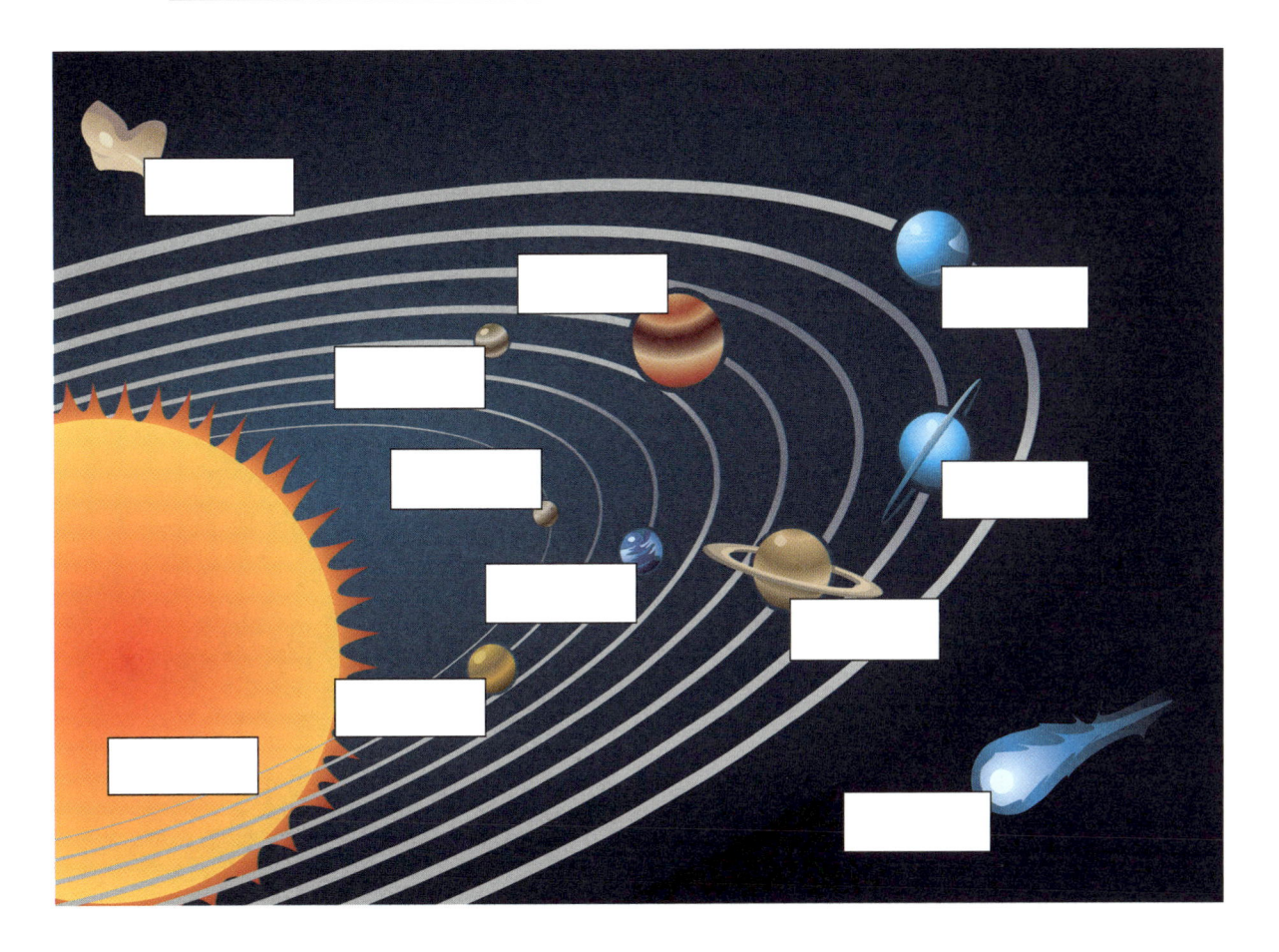

183

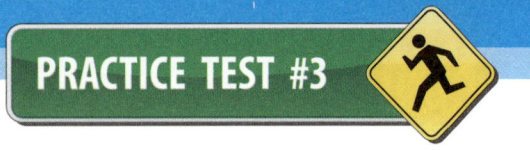

27. Use the word bank to complete the diagram of a volcano.

WORD BANK
volcano   hot magma   side vent   sedimentary rock
crater   metamorphic rock   lava flow   central vault

28. Label the diagram.

Earth's Interior

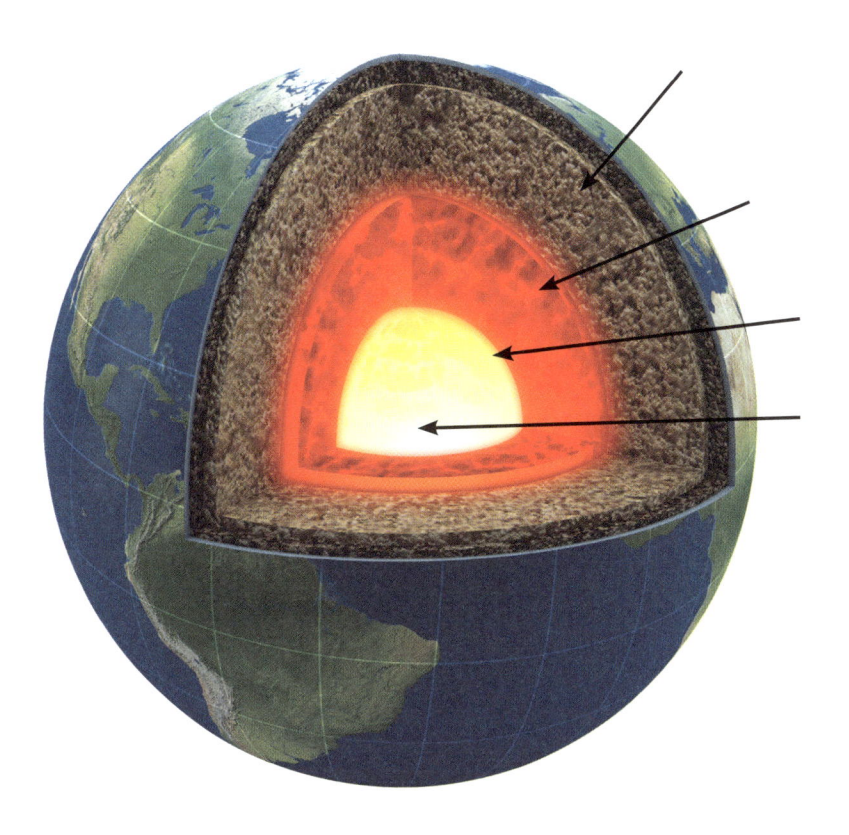

PRACTICE TEST #4

SOCIAL STUDIES

A. Multiple Choice Questions
Choose and circle the best answer.

1. What is the primary language of the United States?
    A. Spanish
    B. English
    C. Chinese
    D. French

2. Which of the following was NOT one of the original thirteen colonies?
    A. California
    B. Pennsylvania
    C. Delaware
    D. Connecticut

3. Which of the following is a cardinal direction?
    A. north
    B. east
    C. south
    D. all of the above

4. Which of the following is the name of a mountain range?
    A. Atlantic
    B. Mississippi
    C. Appalachian
    D. Mexico

B. Context Clues
Read each of the sentences. Use context clues to figure out the meaning of the underlined word. Circle your answer.

5. There are also <u>international</u> conflicts, which are issues that happen with other countries.
    A. local
    B. worldwide
    C. national
    D. neighborhood

6. When any part of our country needs protection from other countries or powers, the Department of Defense sends one or more of these forces to <u>defend</u> the nation.
    A. quit
    B. attack
    C. protect
    D. surrender

7. Each state has at least one elected <u>representative</u>, or person who acts or speaks for the people.
    A. a person that acts for another
    B. an agent
    C. a person that acts for themselves
    D. a group of people

PRACTICE TEST #4

8. The states also have unique <u>natural resources</u> that are found there.
    A. resources that are not renewable
    B. resources made by man
    C. resources that are renewable
    D. resources created by nature

C. True or False Questions
Read each statement. If it is true, write *T* on the line. If it is false, write *F* on the line.

____ 9. The city council is part of the legislative branch of a local government.

____ 10. To make decisions for the community, the city council will only discuss what to do.

____ 11. Every city in the United States has exactly the same number of council members.

____ 12. City council members are elected to their position by vote of the local community members.

D. Matching
Match the explorer to the country he explored for.

____ 13. Francisco Vasquez de Coronado A. Spain

____ 14. Samuel de Champlain B. Spain

____ 15. John Cabot C. Spain

____ 16. Henry Hudson D. England

____ 17. Ponce de Leon E. England

____ 18. Amerigo Vespucci F. France

E. Fill in the Blank
Read each statement. Choose the correct word from the word bank to complete the sentence.

WORD BANK
citizen responsibility right taxes

19. Everybody has the _____ to be treated fairly.

20. A _____ is a duty, or something you are expected to do.

21. Each person is a _____, or official member of the community.

22. Paying _____ is a responsibility of American citizens.

F. Labeling Diagrams
Use the words in the word box to correctly label the parts of the three branches of the United States government.

WORD BANK

Supreme Court   Executive   Legislative   Judicial   Constitution

Congress   President   House of Representatives   Vice President   Senate

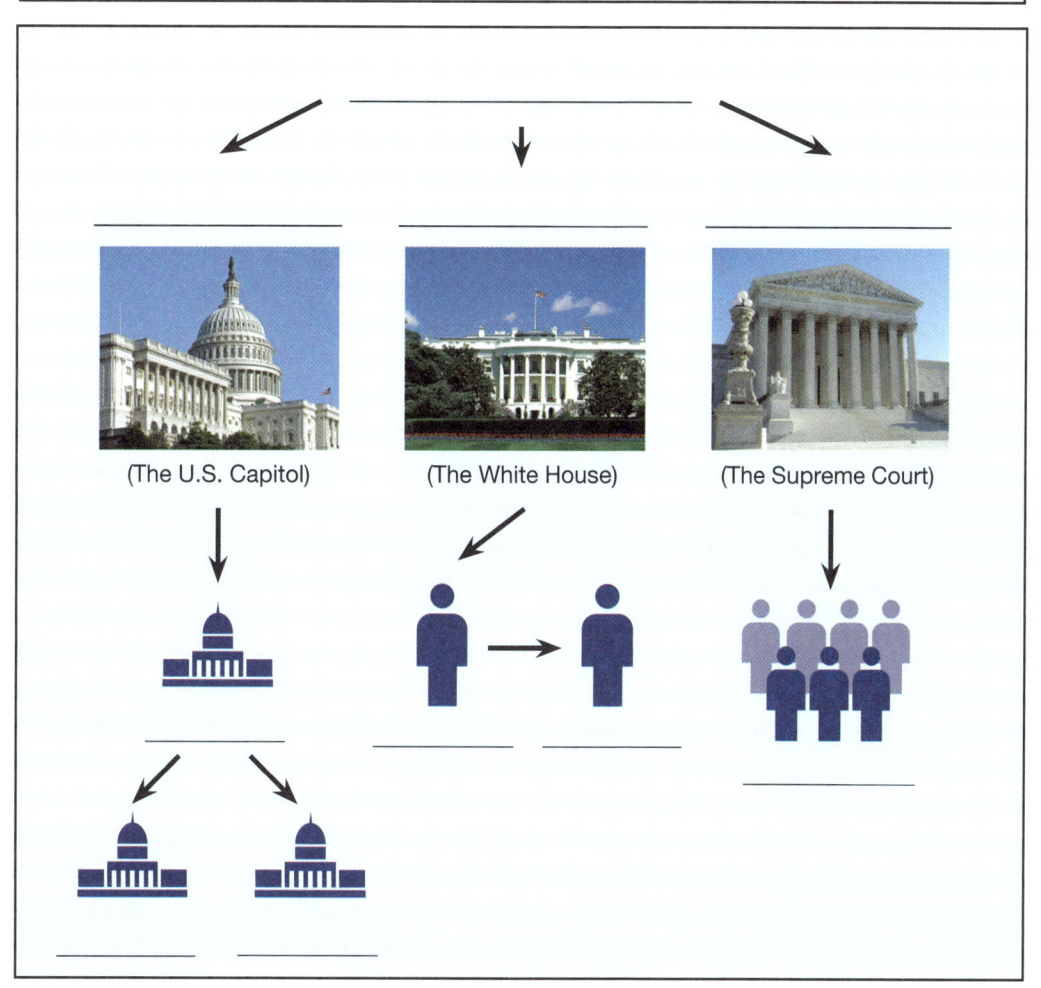

A. Read the myth below. Then, answer the open-ended question.

Pandora
adapted by Sarah Marino

One day long ago, Zeus, the leader of the gods on Mount Olympus, ordered two brothers to go to earth. Their names were Prometheus and Epimetheus. Zeus told the brothers to create man and animals and to give them strengths to help them survive.

Prometheus set out to create man. He worked patiently and carefully, molding man out of clay and water near a riverbed. Epimetheus, meanwhile, worked in a hurry. He gave the animals great powers, such as skill in hunting, speed, keen eyesight, and for some, wings to fly. But Epimetheus forgot that man, too, would need special power to survive on earth.

When Prometheus learned that his brother had given the animals the best of the powers, he grew very angry.

"I created man to be a godlike figure," shouted Prometheus. "You have ruined the plan by giving the animals the greatest powers."

"But, brother, perhaps man and animals can share these powers," Epimetheus replied. He bowed his head, ashamed of his mistake.

"Share? As true as that may be, man still needs his own great power…" Prometheus's voice softened as he tried to think of such a power. He sat at the river's edge and looked toward the sun. Several minutes passed. Then Prometheus clasped his hands together. He shouted, "That's it! Man shall gain fire!"

"How will you get fire from Mount Olympus?" asked Epimetheus. "Zeus does not let any but the mightiest gods have the wonders of fire."

"I will find a way," said Prometheus. "To repay me for your mistake, you must stay here and keep man safe until I return. I am going to Mount Olympus."

Epimetheus agreed, and Prometheus disappeared into the sky.

Zeus kept the fire of Mount Olympus burning day and night. The fire was held in a gigantic torch, beside the great golden fountain. Two one-eyed monsters guarded the flame. Prometheus knew he would need help in getting around them. He called on his friend, the wise goddess Athena. With her aid, Prometheus was able to steal a piece of the flame.

Prometheus then returned to his brother on earth. The brothers showed man how to build a fire. Then they taught him how to roast food over the flame.

Soon Zeus could see that man had gained the power of fire. Zeus became angry and decided to punish Prometheus and man. He created a plan and set out to complete it.

First, Zeus told his son Hephaestus to create a woman to go with man. The son created a beautiful mold from the marble of Mount Olympus. He gave the statue the features of the goddesses. Athena blew wit into the statue's ear and made the woman come to life. Aphrodite kissed her cheek and gave her the power of love. The other gods gave her gifts as well, including kindness and feeling. Zeus gave her the gift of unending curiosity. He named her Pandora.

Zeus took Pandora to earth. He presented her as a bride for Epimetheus. Prometheus had told him that Zeus should not be trusted. But Epimetheus did not want to be punished, so he accepted Pandora into his home.

Before Zeus left Pandora, he gave her a small, oddly shaped clay jar with a sealed lid. He told her that it was her duty to protect the jar. He warned her that she should *never* open it. Pandora agreed, thinking it would be an easy task.

Epimetheus began to adore Pandora's beauty, wit, and kindness. Pandora started to admire her husband as well, and they lived happily, for a time. But Pandora's curiosity would not let her stop thinking of the jar. She carried it with her at all times. Then she realized how much it was taking over her thoughts. She decided to put the jar in the kitchen. It seemed to call to her, though: *Pandora, don't you wonder what I am? Why did Zeus put me in your care? I must be special. Perhaps you could open me and find out?*

Pandora did not know what to do. She tried telling Epimetheus, but he did not understand. He believed that she would obey Zeus.

PRACTICE TEST #5

  Finally, after weeks of wondering, Pandora thought, "I suppose it couldn't hurt if I just peek inside." She took the jar and stepped out of the house. She wanted to be in the sunshine and away from her husband. She began to pull on the lid. It loosened easily. She sighed, and slowly, lifted the lid off of the jar. A great gust of bitterly cold wind blasted out of the jar. Pandora shrieked as it pushed her face. In the stream of wind, she saw many ugly figures emerge and float into the sky: Fear, Jealousy, Anger, Sadness, Gossip, Lies, Blame, Hate—every bad feeling and behavior that man had not yet known. Pandora had just put these bad things onto the earth. Tears began to pour down her face as she tried to put the lid back on the jar. With a great push, she replaced the lid just in time to stop Hope from spilling out. "If Hope had been released, those other awful things would surely have destroyed it," she thought.

  Pandora sat down on the ground, holding the jar to her chest with shaking hands. She felt a heavy sadness because of the horrible things that were now in the world. Then, after a few moments, hope crept into her heart. She began to think that it might not be so bad. "As long as we have hope," she thought, "we can fight those evil things and keep happiness alive."

Compare and contrast the brothers Prometheus and Epimetheus. Tell how they are similar and how they are different. Give at least three examples of how they are the same and how they are different.

PRACTICE TEST #5

B. A Girl Scout troop was surveyed on what activity they wanted to do at the end of the year. Their answers are below. Create a graph below to show their responses. You can make any type of graph you would like: bar graph, tally chart, pictograph, or line plot. Make sure each axis is labeled, and each piece of data is on the chart.

> Sleepover at the science center: 12
> Horseback riding: 13
> Picnic in the park: 8
> Trip to the amusement park: 7

C. Match the noun to its matching plural noun. Not all of the choices will be used.

____ 1. peach
____ 2. box
____ 3. bush
____ 4. church
____ 5. fox
____ 6. wish
____ 7. buzz

A. churches
B. foxs
C. wishes
D. bushes
E. buzzes
F. peaches
G. wishs
H. peach's
I. boxes
J. buzzs
K. foxes

D. Read each question and select the correct answer.

1. What is the head of a town or city called?
   A. president
   B. council member
   C. mayor
   D. captain

PRACTICE TEST #5

2. Which is one of the ways a community provides a way for people to have food?
    A. grocery stores
    B. libraries
    C. gas stations
    D. hair dresser

3. Which of the following is a task that a store clerk might do?
    A. clean the store
    B. help customers
    C. count money in the register
    D. all of the above

4. Which of the following could be considered recreation?
    A. going to work
    B. playing at the park
    C. going grocery shopping
    D. filling the gas tank.

5. Name something that public works does NOT do.
    A. repair potholes
    B. fix street lights
    C. deliver mail
    D. collect garbage

E. Fill in the blank with the correct word from the word bank.

WORD BANK
gold   quartz   crystal   glass   silicon

1. _____ is the second most common element in the earth's crust.
2. Computer chips, circuits, solar cells, and other electronic devices are made with _____.
3. A very flexible metal, _____, is used to make electronics because it can conduct electricity.
4. Quartz is used in the making of _____ and porcelain.
5. A quartz _____ is used in watch batteries.

END OF SECTION TWO

SECTION THREE

ANSWERS

ANSWERS: TEST #1
LANGUAGE ARTS

A. Multiple Choice Questions

1. C. This is the correct choice because in the first paragraph, the author clearly states that the US government is responsible for the care and upkeep of all national parks. After reading this question, you would want to go back, reread the first paragraph, find the answer, and underline it.

2. B. This is the correct answer because the question asks how these two are similar or the same, and choice B was the only one that had a similarity. The other answer choices talked about the differences between the two parks. You could also look back to the second paragraph to find this answer.

3. A. This is the correct choice because it is the only fact. A fact is something you can prove. The other three choices are all opinions. You would not be able to prove, or look up opinions.

4. C. This is the correct answer because the reading passage is set up to discuss how the two places are the same and how they are different. The author gives many facts and does not try to persuade, or tell readers what they should think or believe.

B. Using Context Clues

5. B. This is the correct answer because *ordinary* means normal. The phrase *bored with common life* helps you to figure out the definition.

6. D. This is correct choice because *grateful* means thankful. You can use the word *help* to give you an idea of what grateful might mean. You would not be unhappy, jealous, or rude if someone gave you help.

7. C. This is the correct answer because *stunning* means very pretty. The word *beautiful* can help give you a clue that stunning is another way to say something is pretty.

8. A. Another word for *flaw* is imperfection. The word *weakness* and the example that Midas does not think ahead give you hints that a flaw is the same as an imperfection.

C. True or False Questions

9. True. This is true because all sentences have to have punctuation like a period, question mark, or exclamation point at the end.
10. False. This sentence is false because nouns describe people, places, and things, not actions.
11. False. An exclamatory sentence shows excitement. An interrogative sentence asks a question.
12. True. This is true because verbs are the action words in a sentence.
13. True. All proper nouns must start with a capital letter.

D. Matching

D 14. curiosity
G 15. mature
A 16. aide
H 17. elderly
C 18. mutt
B 19. negotiate
E 20. fetch
F 21. obedient

ANSWERS: TEST #1

E. Fill in the Blank

22. Wilbur is saved from death by <u>Fern</u>, who takes care of him like a baby.
23. The main character in *Charlotte's Web* is <u>Wilbur</u>, who Charlotte describes as a "Some Pig".
24. <u>Avery</u> is Fern's loud and rude brother.
25. The spider who writes in her web, and becomes Wilbur's friend is <u>Charlotte</u>.
26. <u>Templeton</u> is a rat that loves to eat and steal things.

ANSWERS: TEST #2

MATH

A. Multiple Choice Questions

1. B. This is the correct answer because when these two numbers are added, you will get 256. Each of the other answers is too much, too little, or has the numbers of the correct answer mixed up.

2. D. This is the correct choice because the shape is a rectangle. Each of the other three shapes listed all have four sides, but because two sides are long, and the other two are short, this is a rectangle.

3. B. This the correct answer because there is a 9 in the tens column. The tens column is always the second column from the right.

4. A. This is the correct choice because the pattern is to add 3 or skip count by 3. Answer A is the only answer choice that correctly continues to count by 3.

B. Using Context Clues

5. *How many more than* are the keywords. They mean to subtract. 14 – 7 = 7 fuzzy stickers
6. *In all* are the keywords. They mean to add. 10 + 9 = 19 cars
7. *Are left* are the keywords. They mean to subtract. 13 – 7 = 6 raisins
8. *In all* are the keywords. They mean to add. 3 + 8 = 11 books read

C. Solving Word Problems

9. Rosa and her family are on vacation for two weeks. Rosa's mom has asked Rosa to take pictures of their trip. In the first week, Rosa took (87) pictures. In the second week, she took (132) pictures. How many pictures did she take of their family vacation in all?

    132 + 87 = 219 pictures

10. Evan bought a bag of lollipops. There are (50) lollipops in the bag. He handed out (32) lollipops. How many does he have left?

    50 – 32 = 18 lollipops

D. Solving a Math Open-Ended Problem

One example answer is given.

11. Holly could have used 2 quarters, 2 dimes, and 2 nickels. I know this because 2 quarters is 50¢, adding 2 dimes to this is 70¢, and adding 2 nickels to this is 80¢.

E. True or False Questions

12. False. The shape is not a pentagon. A pentagon has five sides, and this shape has six sides, so it is a hexagon.
13. False. The underlined number is in the hundreds column.
14. True.
15. True.

ANSWERS: TEST #2

F. Matching

D   16. cents
B   17. dollars
E   18. penny
A   19. nickel
F   20. dime
C   21. quarter

G. Fill in the Blank

22. The underlined number is in the <u>hundreds</u> column. <u>3</u>25
22. The underlined number is in the <u>thousands</u> column. 1<u>2</u>,900
22. The underlined number is in the <u>ones</u> column. 82<u>1</u>
22. The underlined number is in the <u>ten thousands</u> column. <u>7</u>9,140
23. The underlined number is in the <u>tens</u> column. 5,1<u>0</u>3

H. Charts and Graphs

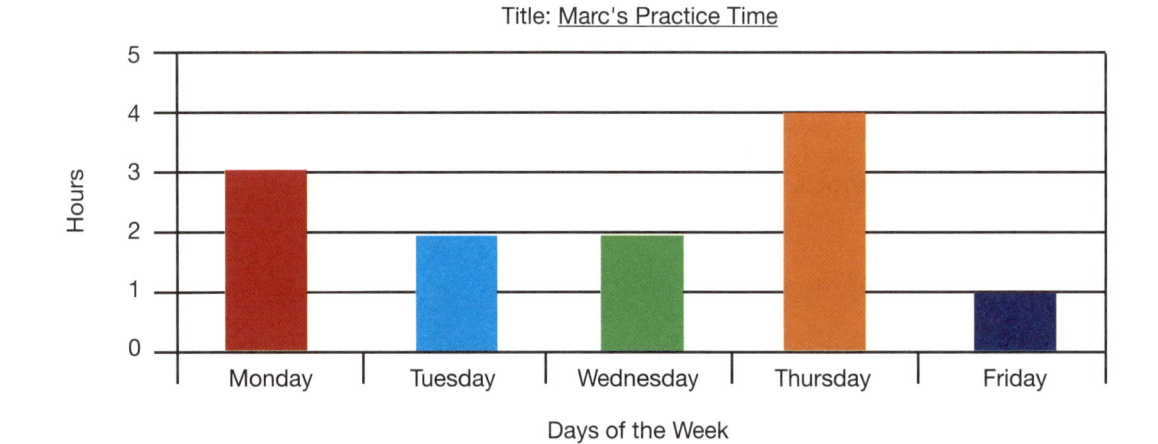

24. Use the data below to make a bar graph.

Marc's Study Time:

Monday: 3 hours
Tuesday: 2 hours
Wednesday: 2 hours
Thursday: 4 hours
Friday: 1 hour

Title: <u>Marc's Practice Time</u>

ANSWERS: TEST #2

25. Use the data below to make a pictograph.

Books read:
Steve: 3
Joe: 6
Michael: 2
Brandon: 4

Title: Books Read

Steve	📙 📙 📙
Joe	📙 📙 📙 📙 📙 📙
Michael	📙 📙
Brandon	📙 📙 📙 📙

📙 = 1 book

26. Use the data to complete the tally chart.

In a survey, kids were asked to choose their favorite drink from the following choices: milk, water, lemonade, and chocolate milk. Their responses are below. Put their answers into a tally chart.

Milk: 9
Water: 6
Lemonade: 7
Chocolate milk: 10

Title: Favorite Drinks

Milk					‌				
Water					‌	
Lemonade					‌		
Chocolate Milk					‌				‌

201

ANSWERS: TEST #2

I. Using Graphs to Answer Questions

27. How many students like spring as their favorite season? 12 students. This is the correct answer because the line for spring goes up to the 12.

28. Which is the favorite season among students? The favorite season among students is summer. This is the correct answer because the bar is the highest out of all of the bars.

29. Which is the least favorite season among students? Winter is the least favorite season. This is the correct answer because its bar is the shortest.

30. How many more students like summer than fall? 4 more students like summer than fall. This is the correct answer because 15 students like summer and 11 students like fall. 15 – 11 = 4 students

31. Which subject is the most popular? Math is the most popular because it has the most student votes, which is 6.

32. How many students combined like science and social studies? 7 students. 4 students liked science and 3 students like social studies. When these were added together, the total is 7 students.

33. Which subject is the least popular? Social studies is the least popular. Only 3 students liked social studies, and that was the smallest number of the four subjects.

34. How many more students like reading than social studies? 2 more students like reading than social studies. 5 students like reading and 3 like social studies. 5 – 3 = 2

ANSWERS: TEST #3 — SCIENCE

A. Multiple Choice Questions

1. A. This is the correct answer because igneous rocks are the only rocks that are formed by cooled lava.
2. B. Humus is a combination of the best minerals and types of soil that provide the most nutrients to grow plants.
3. B. Plates are not one of the layers of the earth. Tectonic plates sit on top of the crust, but they are not one of the layers.
4. C. When two air masses meet, a front develops. Temperature and humidity talk about the conditions in the air.

B. Vocabulary

5. B. You can use the word *revolve* to help you remember that revolutions have to do with things turning and spinning.
6. C. *Prehistoric* means very old. You can use *pre-* to know that means before. Before history would be very old.
7. A. The word *sediment* is part of sedimentary, which would tell you this type of rock is made from sediments.
8. C. You can use what you know about the word *morph* to know that a metamorphic rock is formed from changes.

C. True or False Questions

9. True.
10. False. Sound is created by vibrations in the air.
11. False. Vibrations create waves, and the waves become sound.
12. True.

D. Matching

D 13. observation
A 14. hypothesis
H 15. crystal
C 16. variables
G 17. classify
E 18. streak
F 19. luster
B 20. mineral

E. Fill in the Blank

21. Another name for rain, snow, sleet, and hail is <u>precipitation</u>.
22. A <u>meteorologist</u> is a scientist that studies the weather.
23. The measure of how hot or cold it is is also known as <u>temperature</u>.
24. The <u>weather</u> is the condition of the air at a given time and place.
25. The amount of moisture in the air determines the <u>humidity.</u>

ANSWERS: TEST #3

F. Labeling Diagrams

26. Look at the diagram of the solar system. Use the words in the word bank to help you correctly name each part.

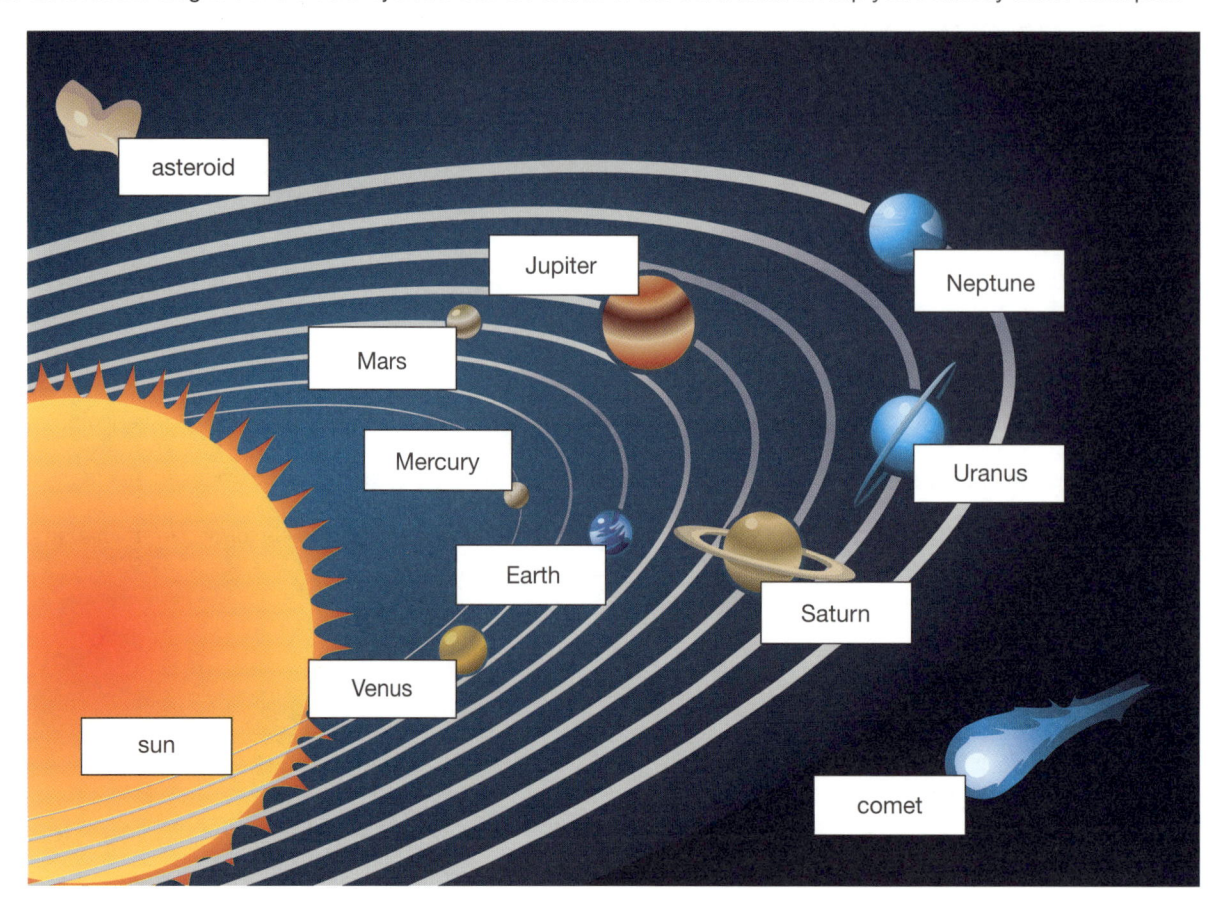

- asteroid
- Jupiter
- Mars
- Neptune
- Mercury
- Uranus
- Earth
- Saturn
- Venus
- sun
- comet

ANSWERS: TEST #3

27. Use the word bank to complete the diagram of a volcano.

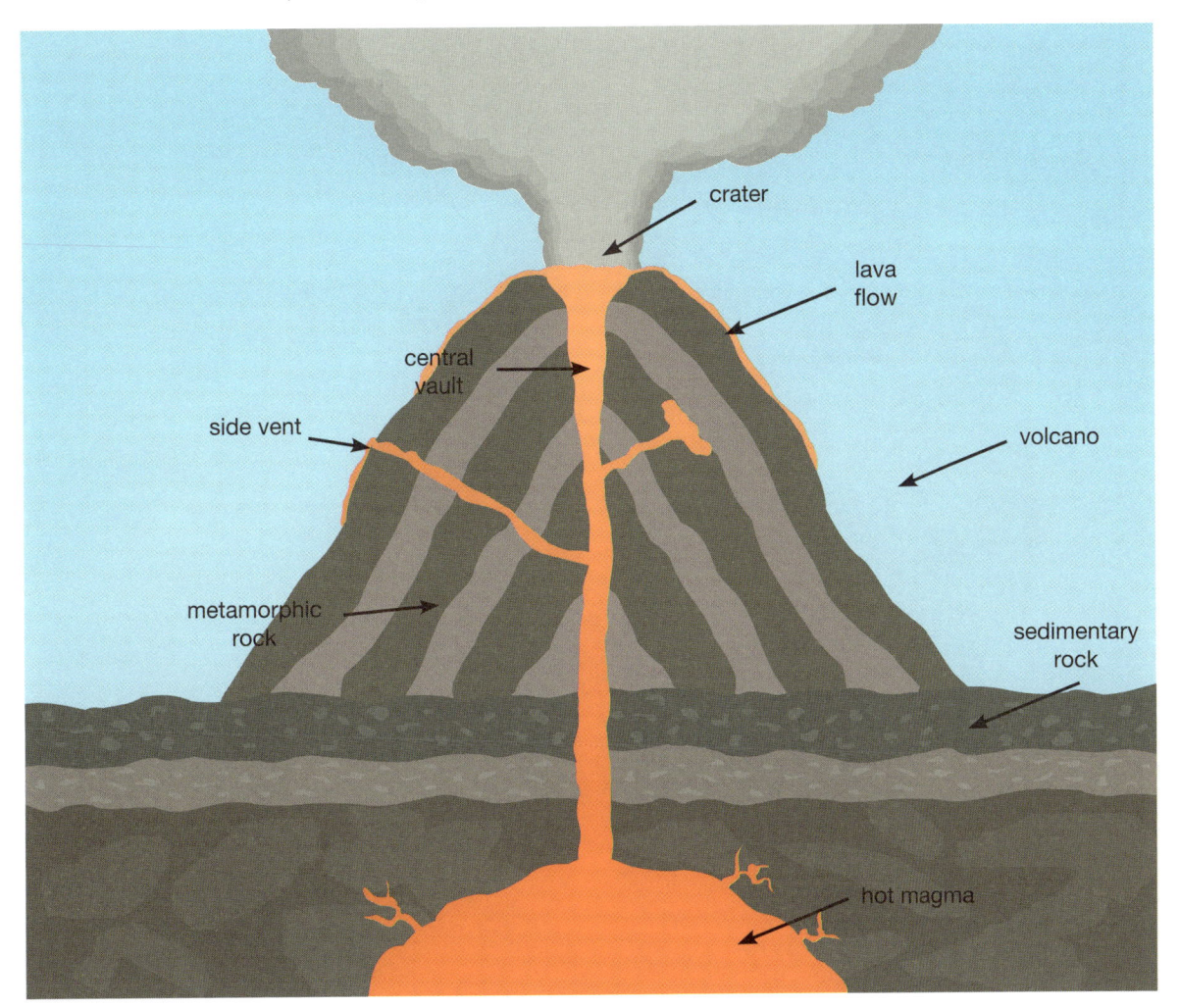

- crater
- lava flow
- central vault
- side vent
- volcano
- metamorphic rock
- sedimentary rock
- hot magma

205

ANSWERS: TEST #3

28. Label the diagram.

Earth's Interior

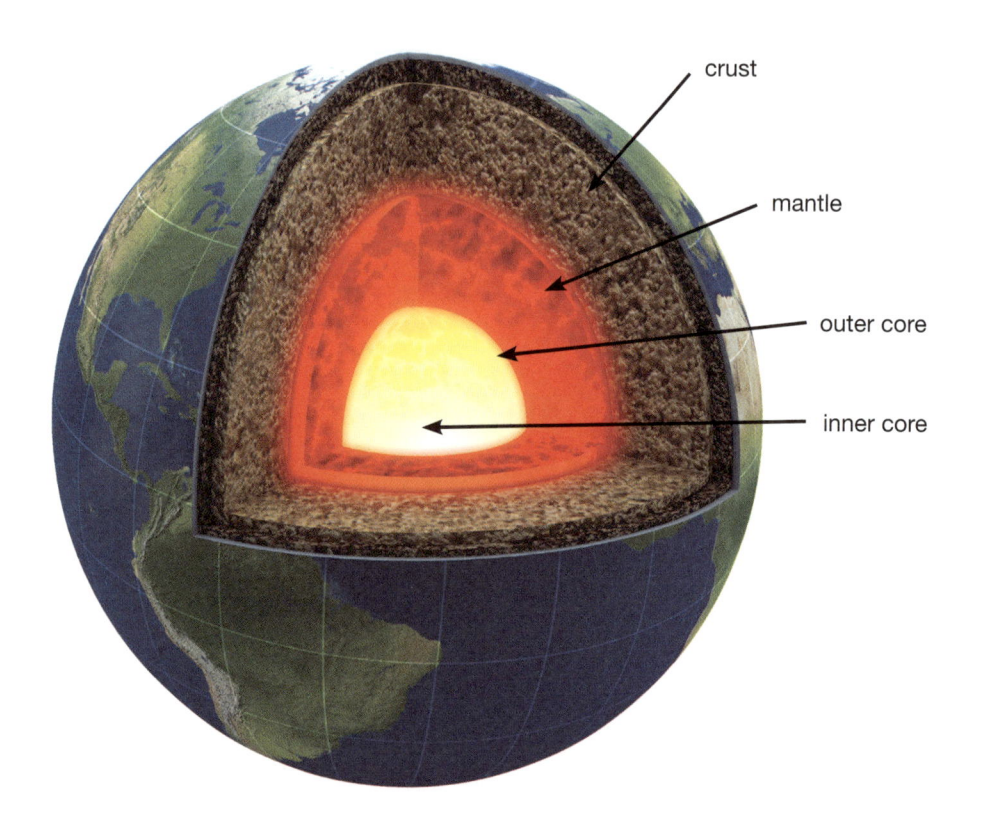

- crust
- mantle
- outer core
- inner core

ANSWERS: TEST #4

SOCIAL STUDIES

A. Multiple Choice Questions

1. B. English is the primary language of the United States. While the other three languages may be spoken by people living in our country, English is the primary language.

2. A. California was not part of the original thirteen colonies. The other three states were part of the colonies

3. D. All three of the choices given are cardinal directions, so all of the above is the best choice.

4. C. Atlantic is the name of an ocean, Mississippi is a river (and a state), and Mexico is the name of a county. Appalachian is the only choice that is the name of a mountain range.

B. Context Clues

5. B. *International* means worldwide. In the sentence, it talks about problems with other countries, which means across the world, and not just in our own country.

6. C. *Defend* means to protect. The word *protecting* at the beginning of the sentence tells you that defend means to protect.

7. A. The end of the sentence gives the definition of this word.

8. D. You can use the words to help you realize that *natural* means in nature.

C. True or False Questions

9. True.
10. False. City council discusses and then votes on what to do to help their community.
11. False. Every city has a different number of city council members, depending on the size of the city.
12. True.

D. Matching

A, B, or C	13. Francisco Vasques de Coronado
F	14. Samuel de Champlain
D or E	15. John Cabot
D or E	16. Henry Hudson
A, B, or C	17. Ponce de Leon
A, B, or C	18. Amerigo Vespucci

E. Fill in the Blank

19. Everybody has the <u>right</u> to be treated fairly.
20. A <u>responsibility</u> is a duty, or something you are expected to do.
21. Each person is a <u>citizen</u>, or official member of the community.
22. Paying <u>taxes</u> is a responsibility of American citizens.

F. Labeling Diagrams

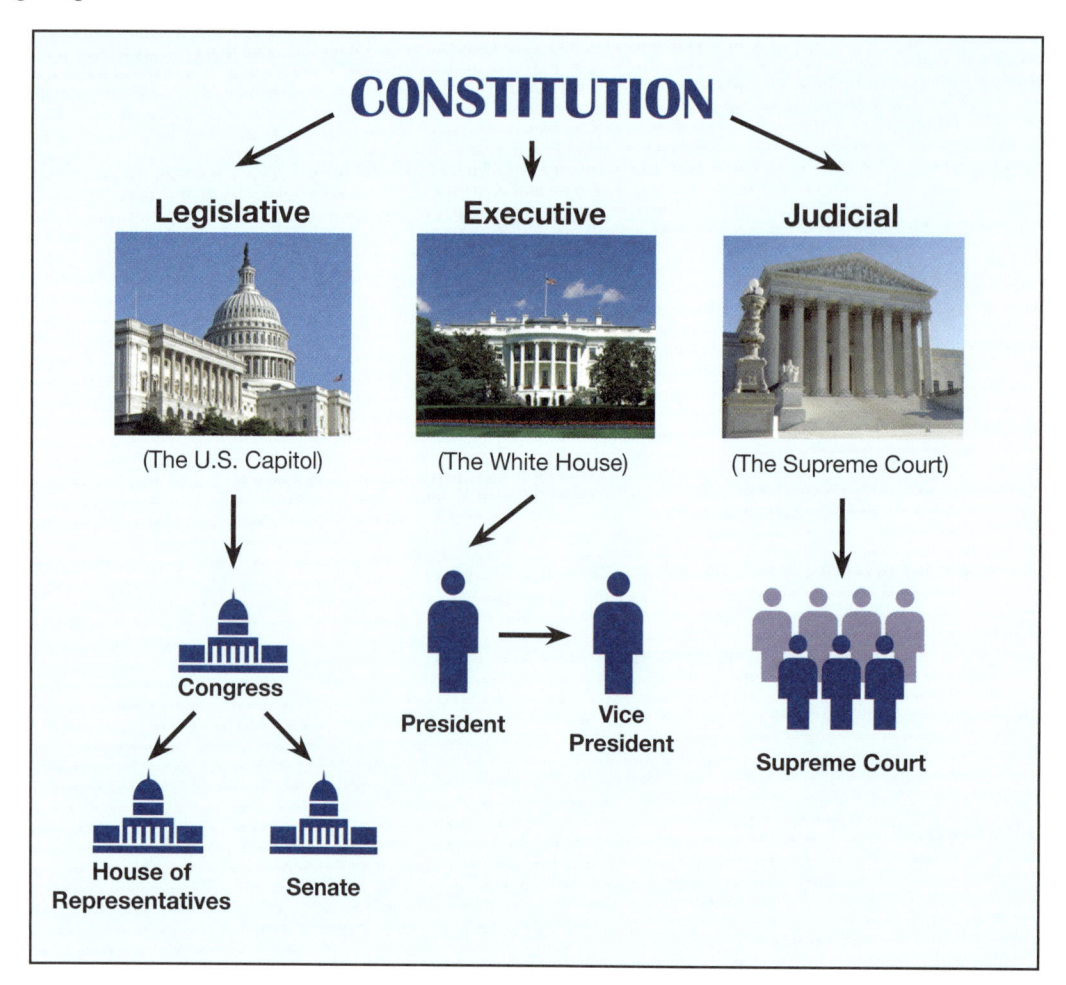

CONSTITUTION

- Legislative (The U.S. Capitol)
  - Congress
    - House of Representatives
    - Senate
- Executive (The White House)
  - President → Vice President
- Judicial (The Supreme Court)
  - Supreme Court

ANSWERS: TEST #5 FINAL

A. Example of an acceptable answer:

    Prometheus and Epimetheus are brothers. In some ways they are similar, but in other easy they are different. Both Prometheus and Epimetheus were creating man and animals. They both forgot to give man enough special powers to survive on the earth. The brothers showed man how to use fire.

    The brothers were different in many ways. Prometheus is very patient and takes his time. Epimetheus is not patient and hurries through his work. Epimetheus gave man the best powers, while Prometheus did not. Prometheus found a way to give man fire, while Epimetheus stayed behind to keep man safe.

B. Your student can choose any type of graph he would like. The example is given as a bar graph.

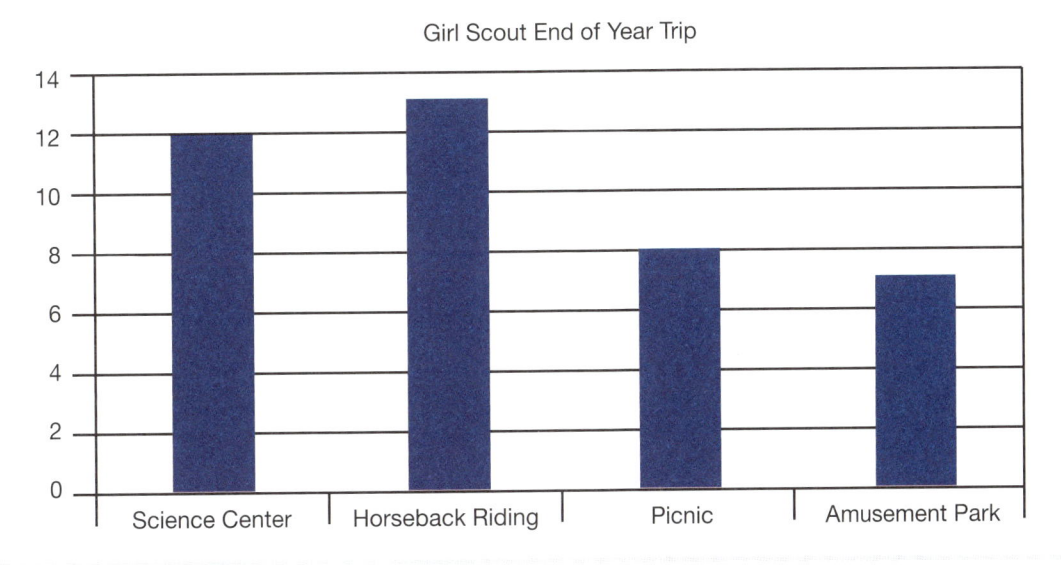

Girl Scout End of Year Trip

Activity	Count
Science Center	12
Horseback Riding	13
Picnic	8
Amusement Park	7

C. The general rule for making a noun plural when it ends in -zz, -x, -sh, or -ch is to add -es to the ending.

F   1. peach
I   2. box
D   3. bush
A   4. church
K   5. fox
C   6. wish
E   7. buzz

D. Read each question and select the correct answer

1. C. This is the correct answer because the head of a town or city is called the mayor.

2. A. Grocery stores are one way a community provides a service for community members to get food for their families.

3. D. A store clerk will clean the store, help customers find what they need, and keep track of the money in the cash register.

4. B. Playing in the park is considered recreation because it is something you can do for fun or enjoyment.

5. C. Public works does not deliver the mail. The postal service will deliver mail. Public works will repair potholes, fix street lights, and collect trash.

ANSWERS: TEST #5

E. Fill in the blank with the correct word from the word bank.

1. <u>Silicon</u> is the second most common element in the earth's crust.

2. Computer chips, circuits, solar cells, and other electronic devices are made with <u>quartz</u>.

3. A very flexible metal, <u>gold</u>, is used to make electronics because it can conduct electricity.

4. Quartz is used in the making of <u>glass</u> and porcelain.

5. A quartz <u>crystal</u> is used in watch batteries.

END OF SECTION THREE